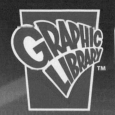

GRAPHIC LIBRARY

GRAPHIC SCIENCE

THE WORLD OF FOOD CHAINS

WITH MAX AXIOM SUPER SCIENTIST

An Augmented Reading Science Experience

by Liam O'Donnell | illustrated by Cynthia Martin and Bill Anderson

Consultant:
Dr. Ronald Browne
Associate Professor of Elementary Education
Minnesota State University, Mankato

CAPSTONE PRESS
a capstone imprint

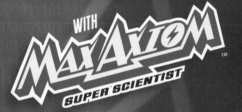

Graphic Library is published by Capstone Press,
1710 Roe Crest Drive, North Mankato, Minnesota 56003.
www.mycapstone.com

Library of Congress Cataloging-in-Publication Data is available on the Library of Congress website.

ISBN: 978-1-5435-2951-7 (library binding)
ISBN: 978-1-5435-2962-3 (paperback)
ISBN: 978-1-5435-2972-2 (eBook PDF)

Summary: In graphic novel format, follows the adventures of Max Axiom as he explains the science behind food chains.

Art Director and Designer
Bob Lentz and Thomas Emery

Colorist
Matt Webb

Cover Artist
Tod Smith

Editor
Donald Lemke

Photo Credits
Capstone Studio/Karon Dubke: 29; iStockphoto Inc./Sandra vom Stein: 10;
Shutterstock/Roux Frederic: 11

This is a Capstone 4D book!

Want fun videos that go with this book?

Just visit www.capstone4d.com

Use this password
food.29517

Printed in the United States 5170

TABLE OF CONTENTS

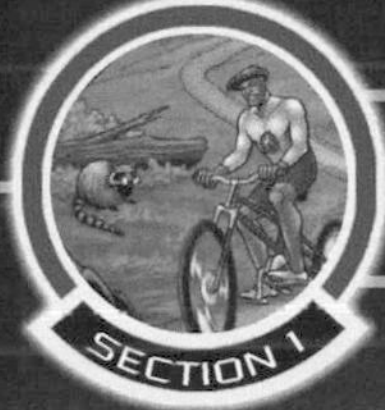
SECTION 1

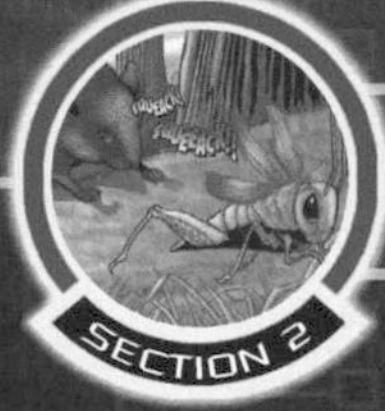
SECTION 2

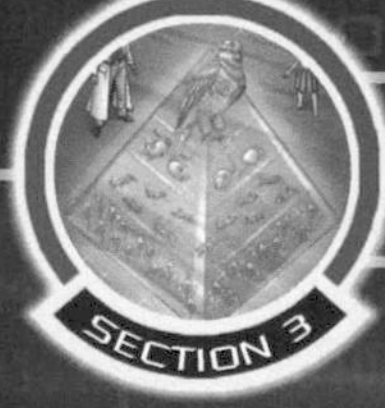
SECTION 3

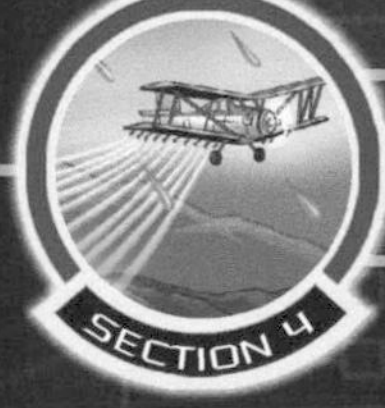
SECTION 4

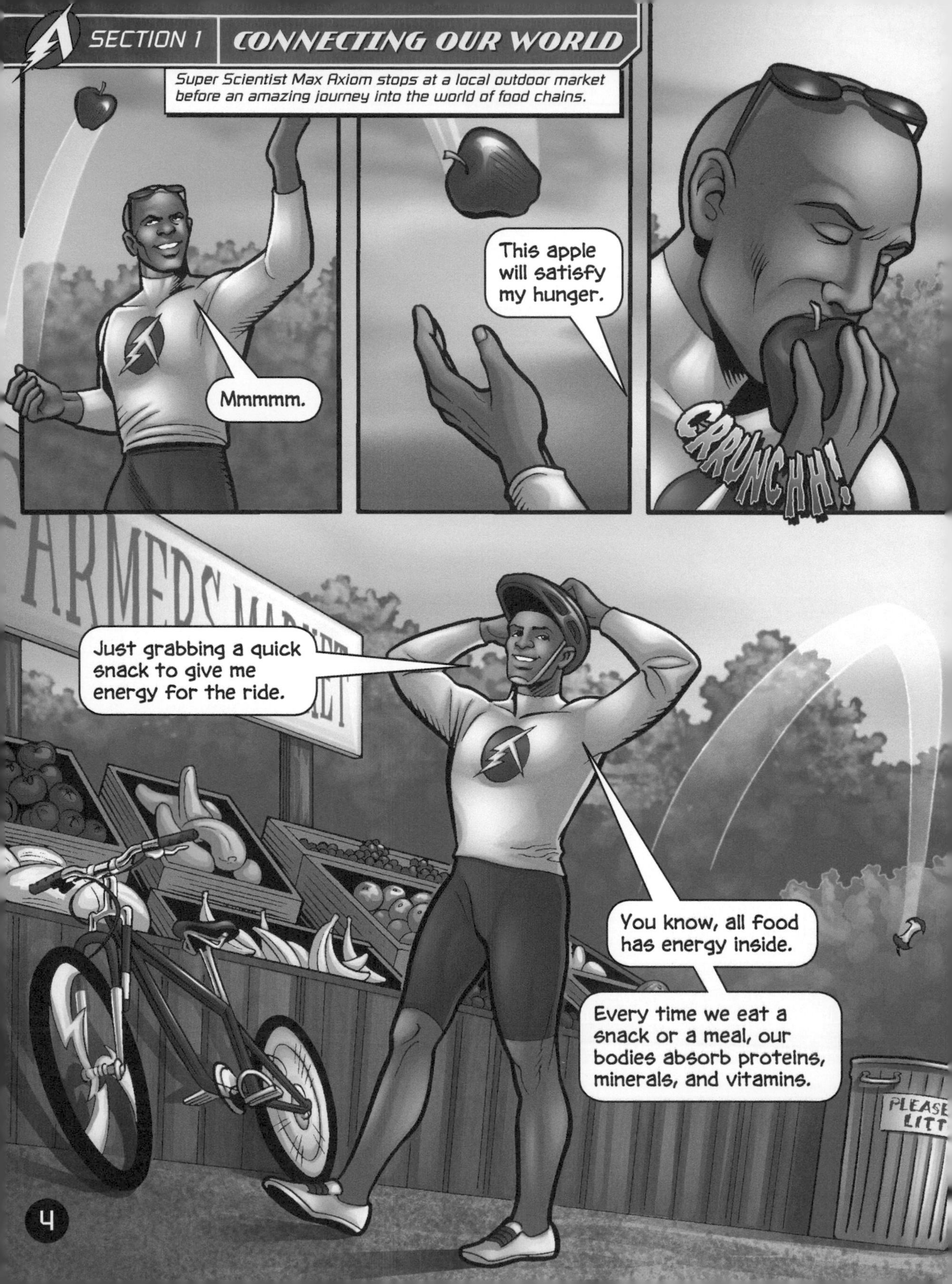
SECTION 1
CONNECTING OUR WORLD
Super Scientist Max Axiom stops at a local outdoor market before an amazing journey into the world of food chains.
Mmmmm.
This apple will satisfy my hunger.
CRRUNCHH!
Just grabbing a quick snack to give me energy for the ride.
You know, all food has energy inside.
Every time we eat a snack or a meal, our bodies absorb proteins, minerals, and vitamins.

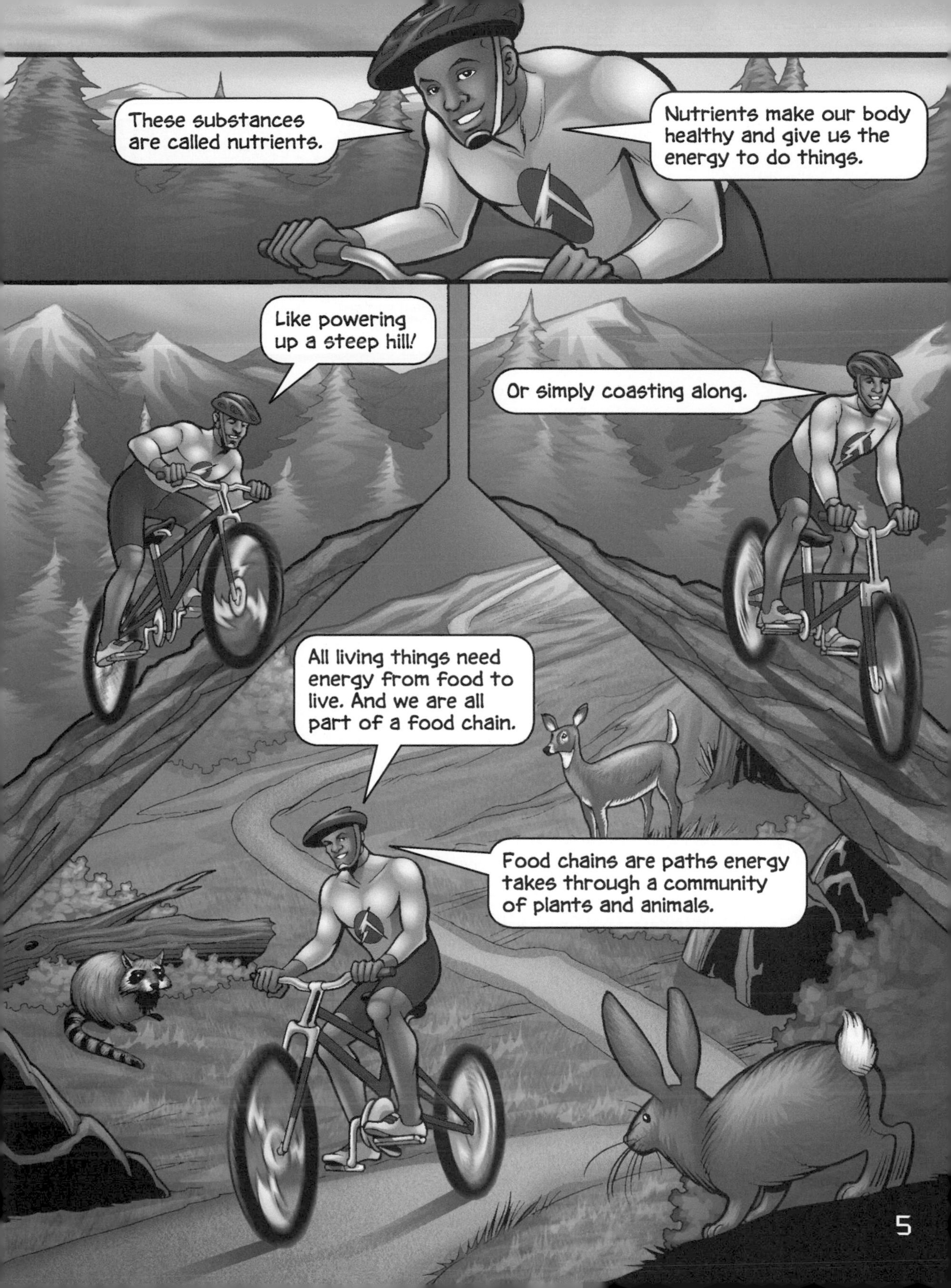
These substances are called nutrients.
Nutrients make our body healthy and give us the energy to do things.
Like powering up a steep hill!
Or simply coasting along.
All living things need energy from food to live. And we are all part of a food chain.
Food chains are paths energy takes through a community of plants and animals.

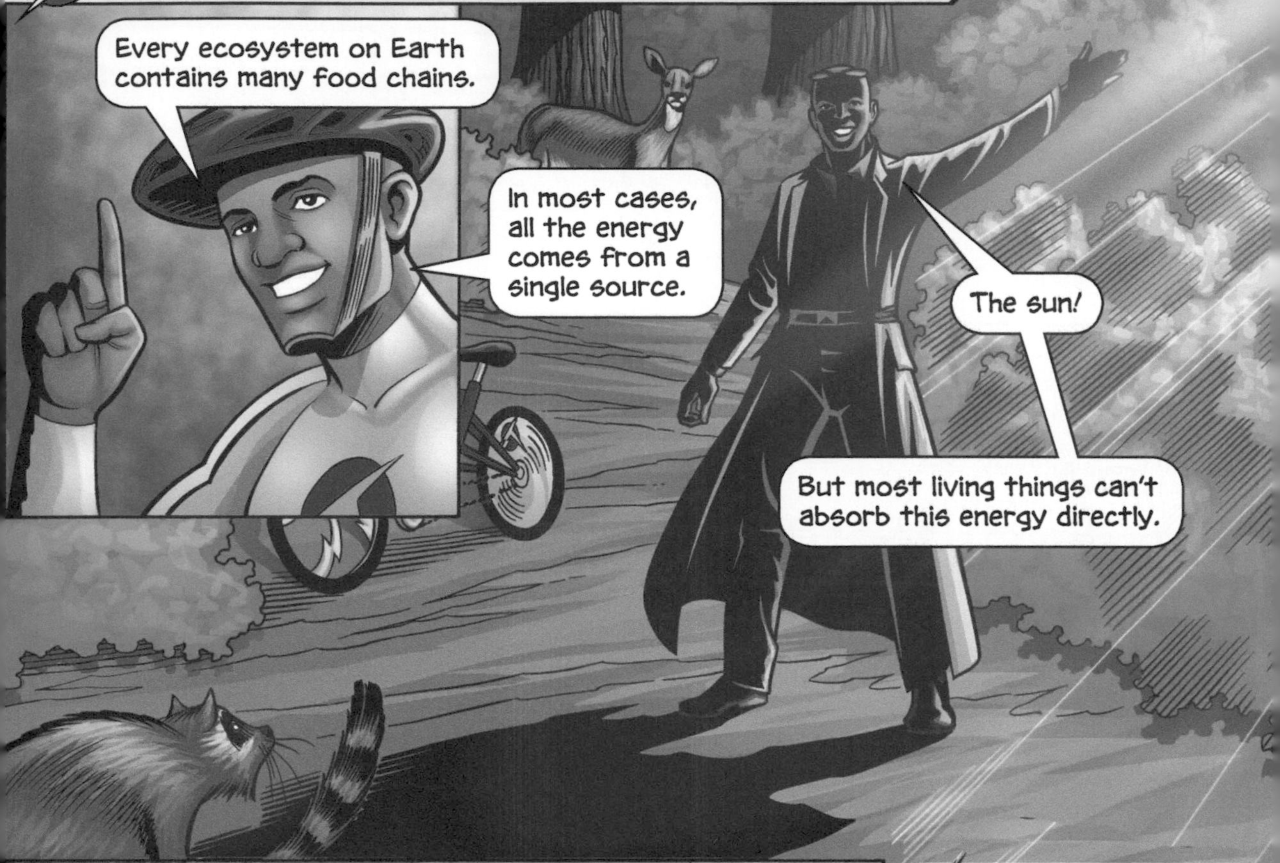
Every ecosystem on Earth contains many food chains.
In most cases, all the energy comes from a single source.
The sun!
But most living things can't absorb this energy directly.

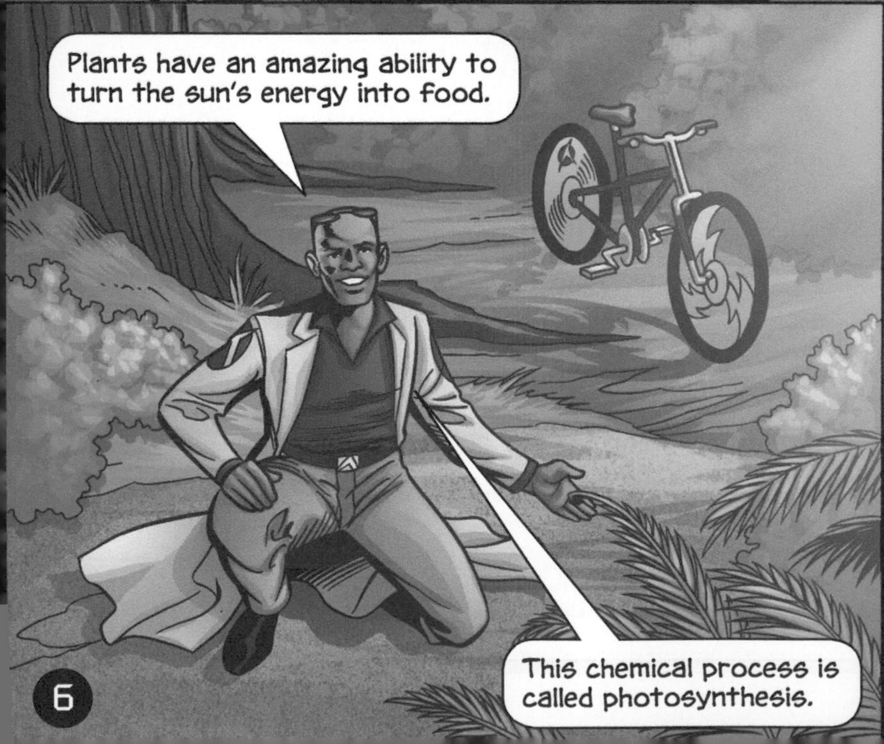
Plants have an amazing ability to turn the sun's energy into food.
This chemical process is called photosynthesis.

DEFINITION

Photosynthesis (foh-toh-SIN-thuh-siss) a chemical process by which green plants make their food; plants use energy from the sun to turn water and carbon dioxide into food, and they give off oxygen as a by-product.

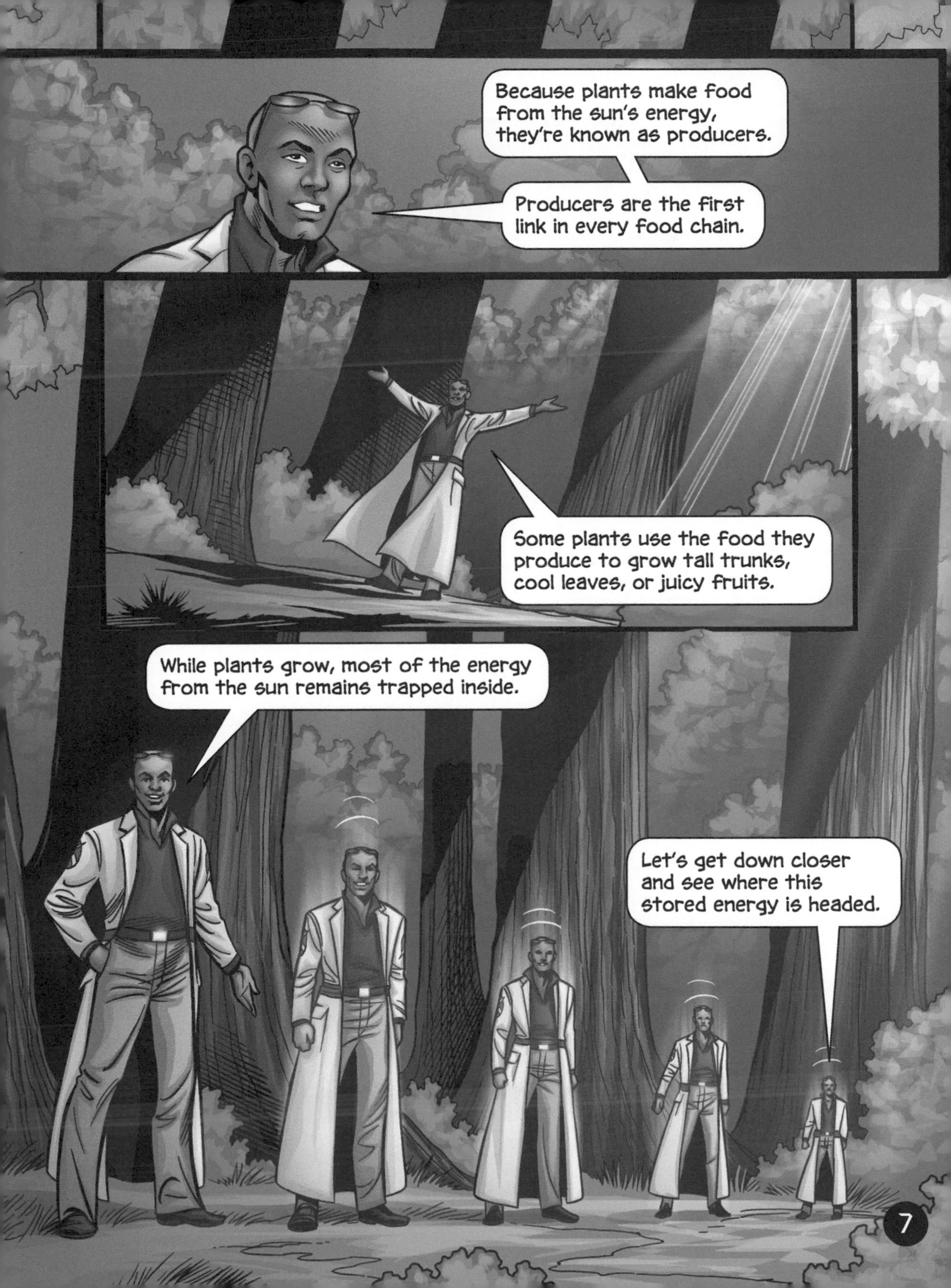
Because plants make food from the sun's energy, they're known as producers.
Producers are the first link in every food chain.
Some plants use the food they produce to grow tall trunks, cool leaves, or juicy fruits.
While plants grow, most of the energy from the sun remains trapped inside.
Let's get down closer and see where this stored energy is headed.

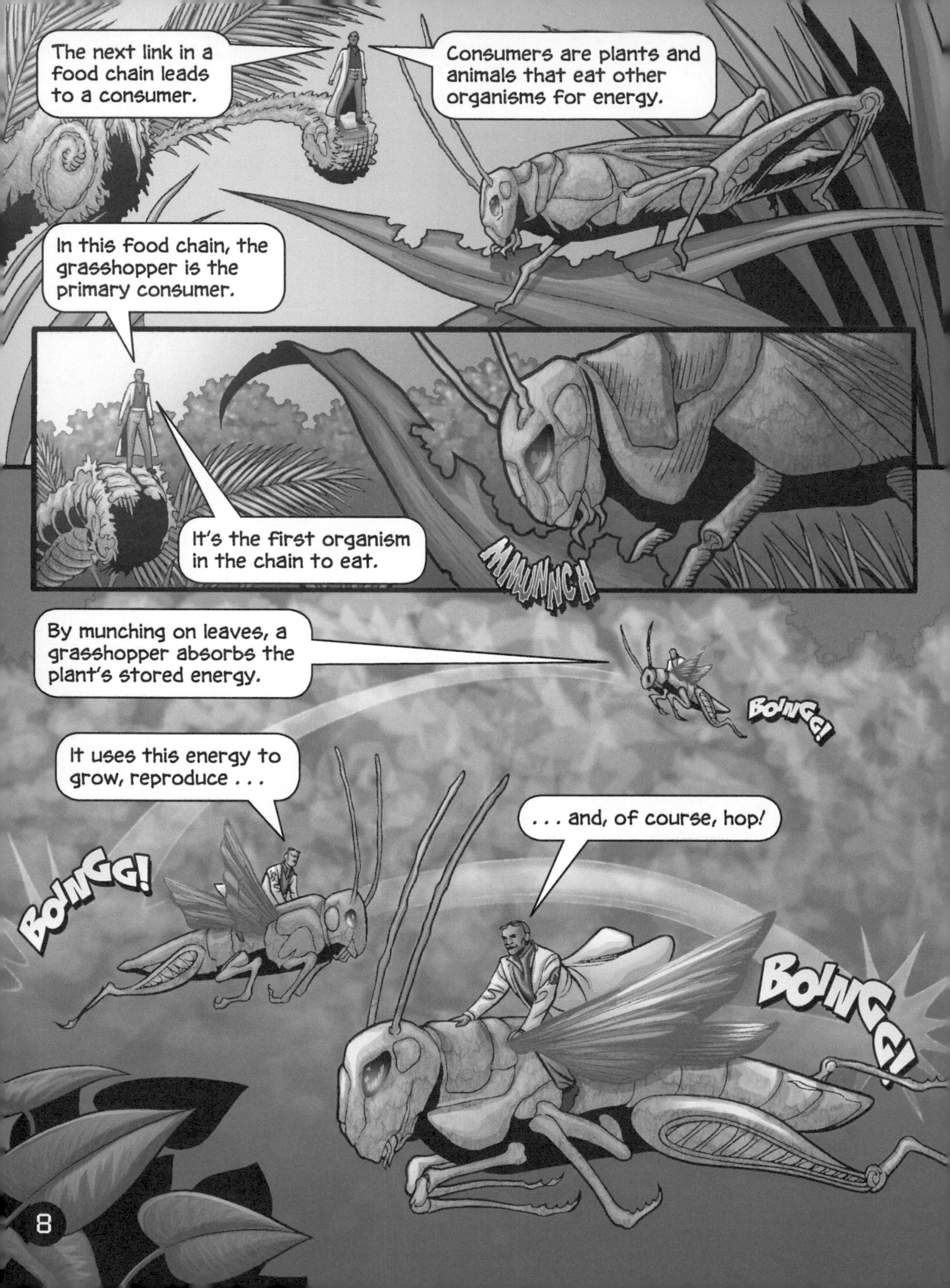

The next link in a food chain leads to a consumer.
Consumers are plants and animals that eat other organisms for energy.
In this food chain, the grasshopper is the primary consumer.
It's the first organism in the chain to eat.
MMUNNCH
By munching on leaves, a grasshopper absorbs the plant's stored energy.
BOINGG!
It uses this energy to grow, reproduce . . .
BOINGG!
. . . and, of course, hop!
BOINGG!

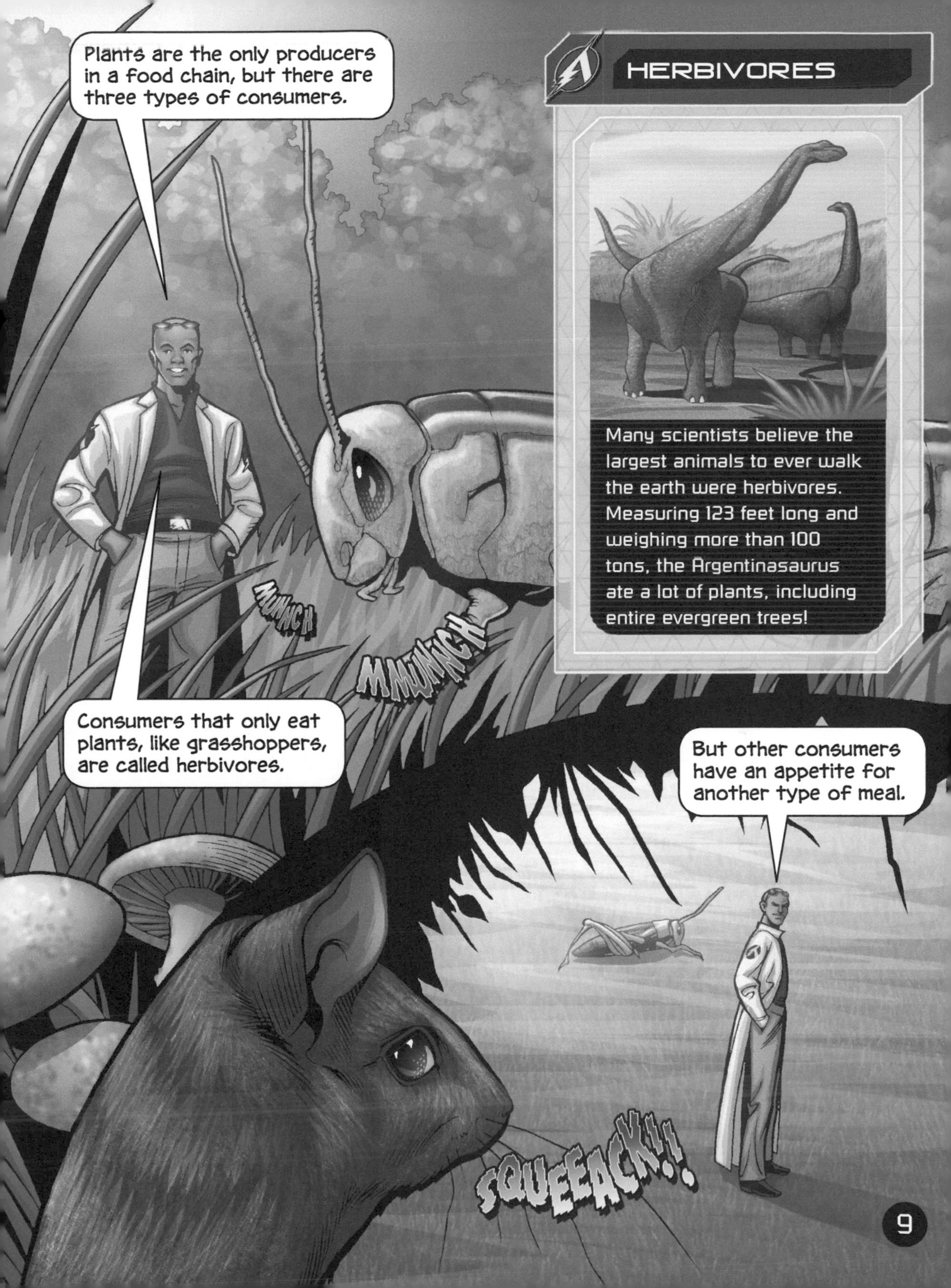
Plants are the only producers in a food chain, but there are three types of consumers.
HERBIVORES
Many scientists believe the largest animals to ever walk the earth were herbivores. Measuring 123 feet long and weighing more than 100 tons, the Argentinasaurus ate a lot of plants, including entire evergreen trees!
MUNNCH
MMUNNCH
Consumers that only eat plants, like grasshoppers, are called herbivores.
But other consumers have an appetite for another type of meal.
SQUEEACK!!!

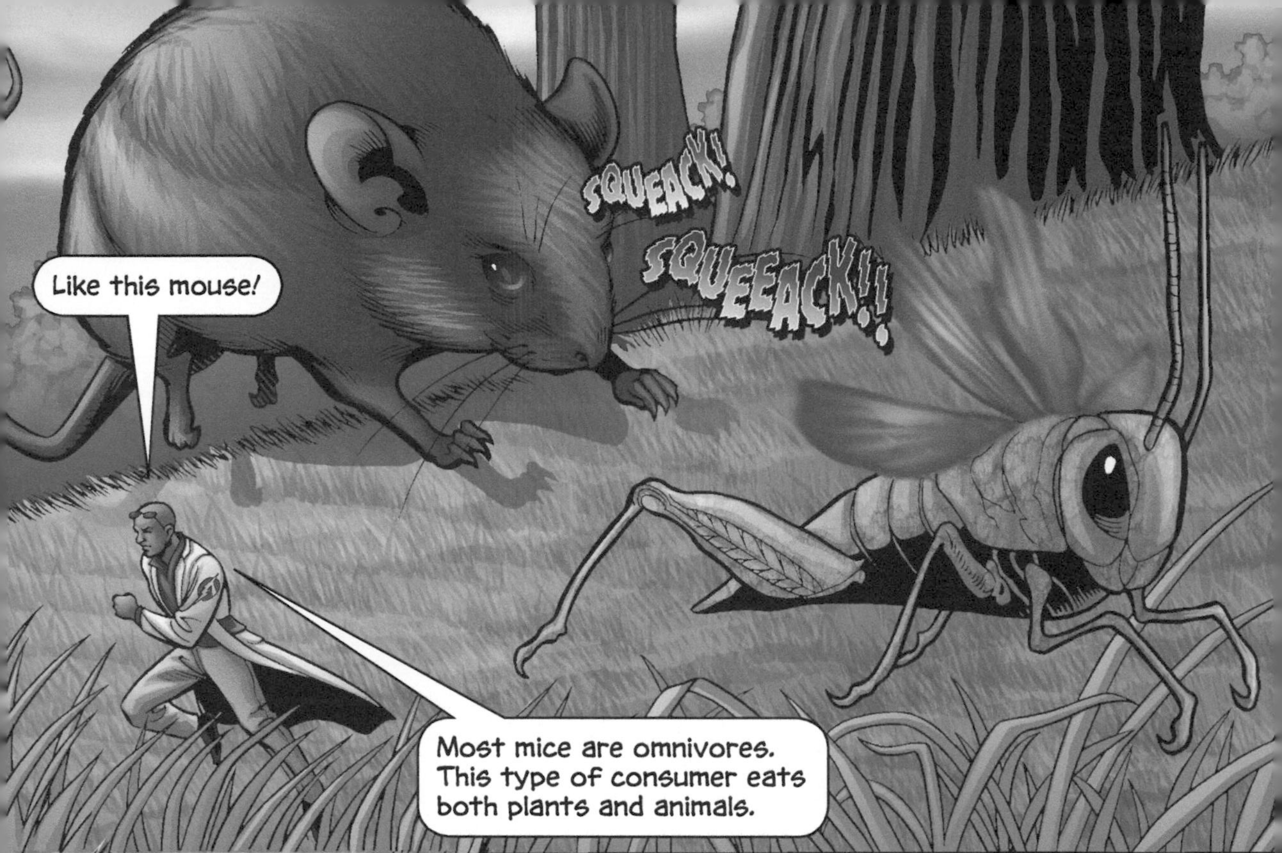
Like this mouse!
SQUEACK!
SQUEEACK!!
Most mice are omnivores. This type of consumer eats both plants and animals.

OMNIVORES

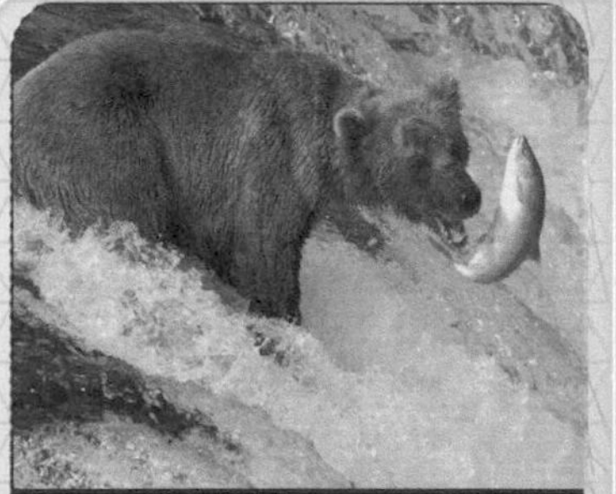

Many animals and insects eat both plants and other animals. Omnivores include most rodents, chickens, raccoons, and even humans. Kodiak bears are the largest omnivores on land. They fill up on grasses and berries, as well as salmon.

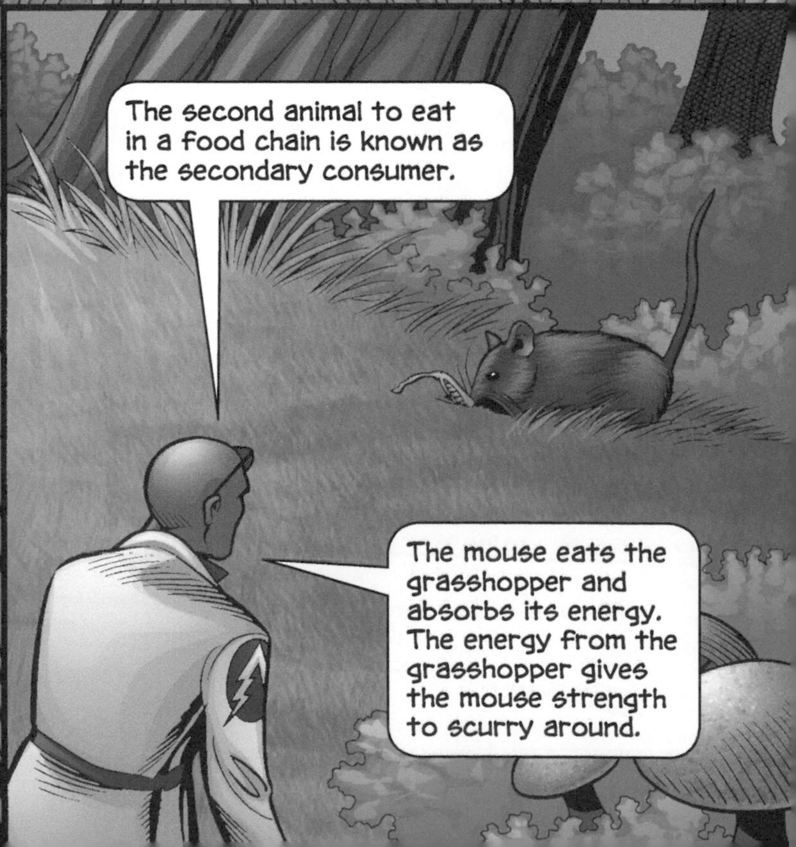
The second animal to eat in a food chain is known as the secondary consumer.
The mouse eats the grasshopper and absorbs its energy. The energy from the grasshopper gives the mouse strength to scurry around.

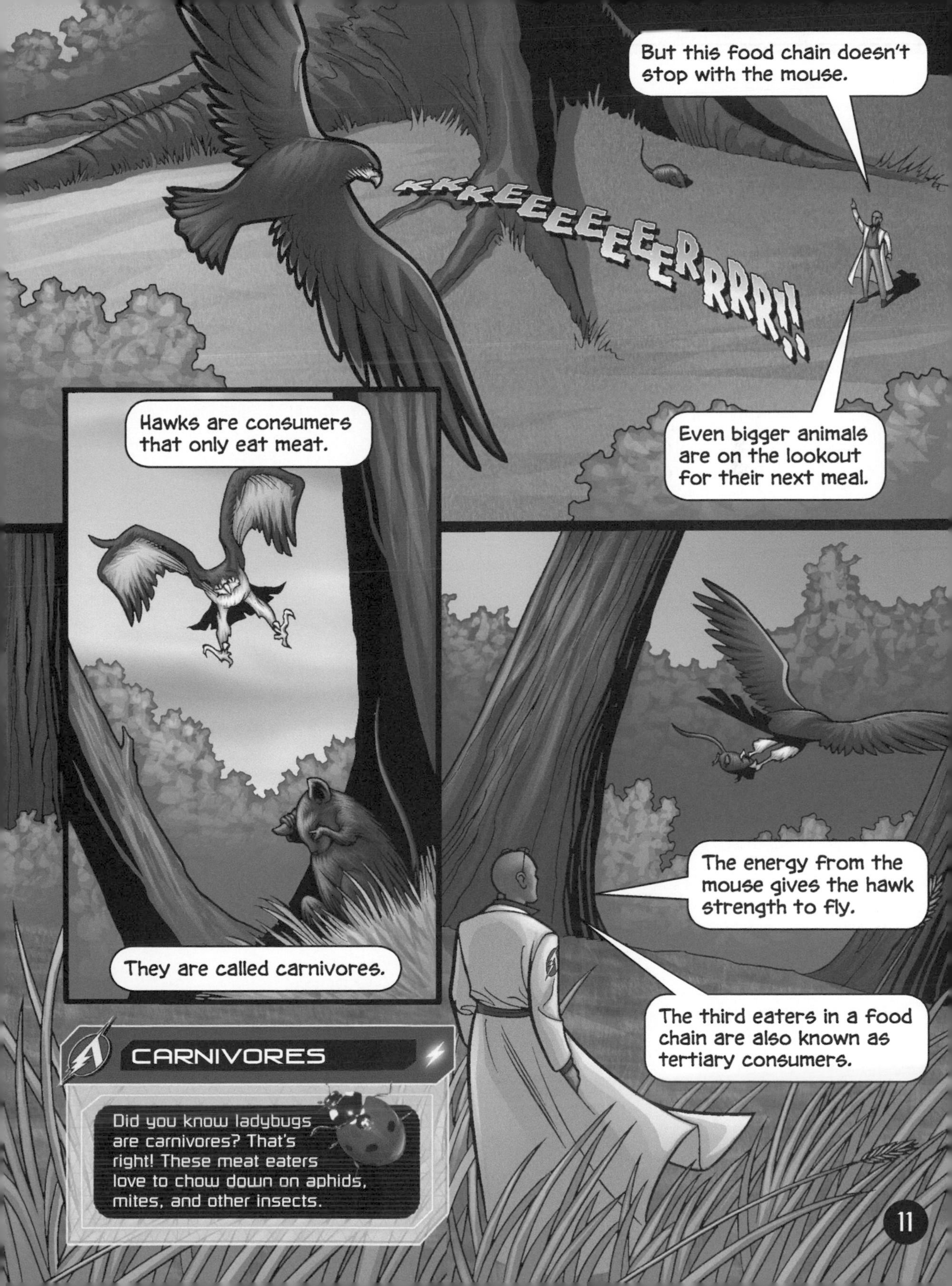
But this food chain doesn't stop with the mouse.
KKKEEEEEEEERRRR!!
Even bigger animals are on the lookout for their next meal.
Hawks are consumers that only eat meat.
They are called carnivores.
The energy from the mouse gives the hawk strength to fly.
The third eaters in a food chain are also known as tertiary consumers.

CARNIVORES

Did you know ladybugs are carnivores? That's right! These meat eaters love to chow down on aphids, mites, and other insects.

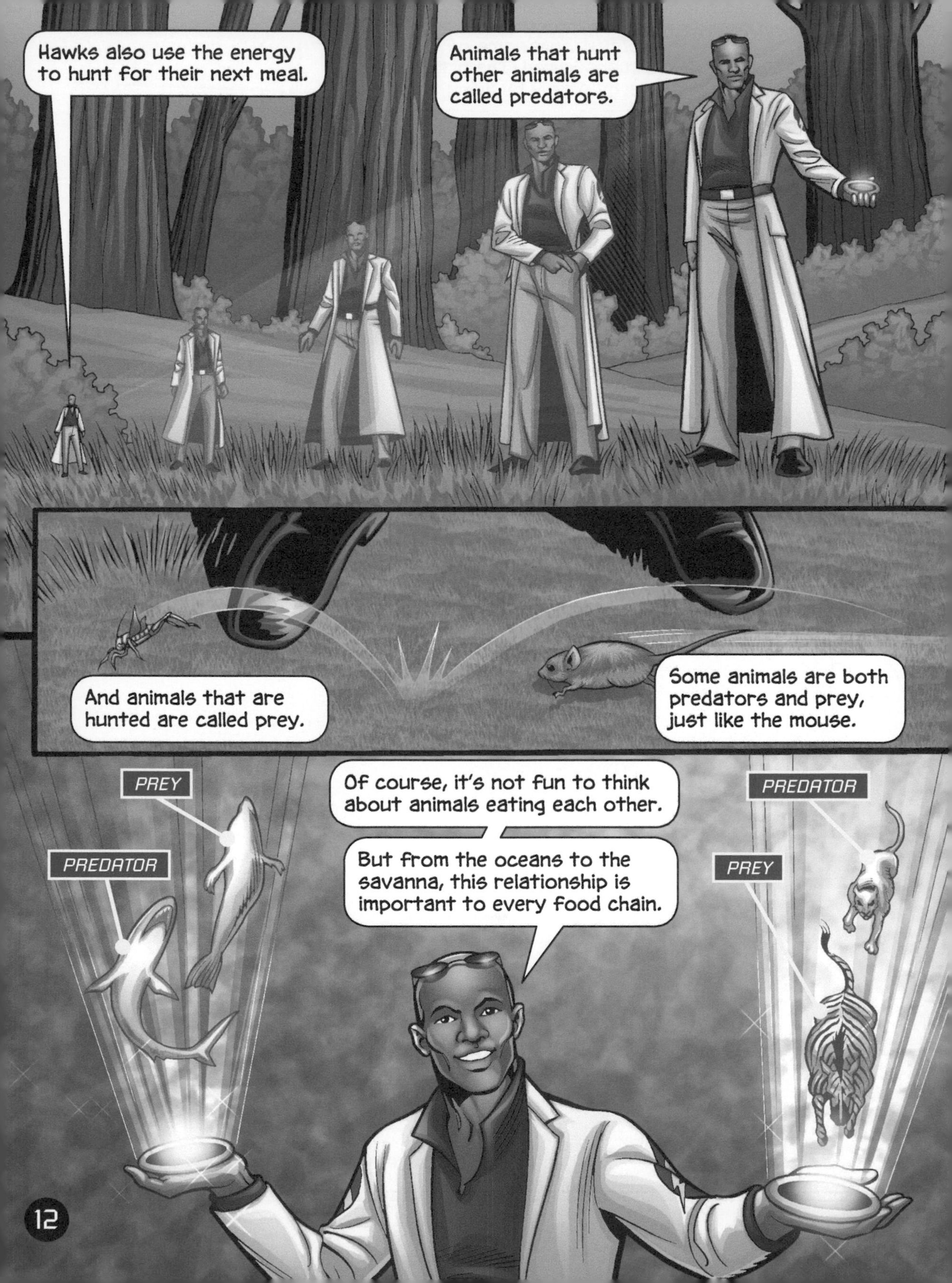
Hawks also use the energy to hunt for their next meal.
Animals that hunt other animals are called predators.
And animals that are hunted are called prey.
Some animals are both predators and prey, just like the mouse.
PREY
PREDATOR
Of course, it's not fun to think about animals eating each other.
But from the oceans to the savanna, this relationship is important to every food chain.
PREDATOR
PREY

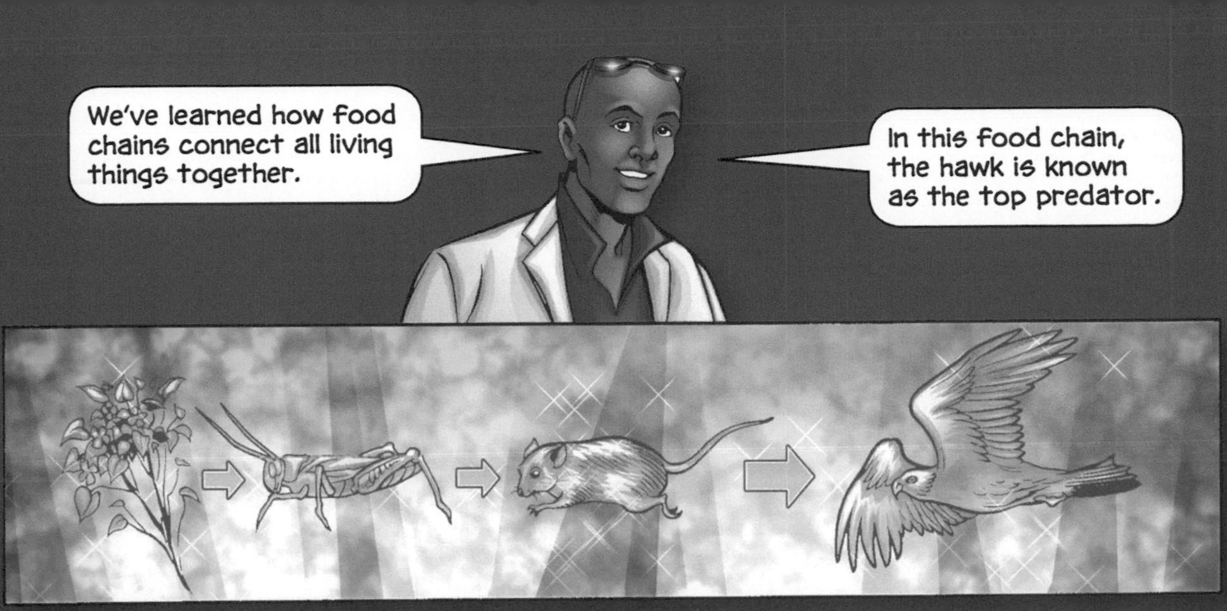
We've learned how food chains connect all living things together.
In this food chain, the hawk is known as the top predator.

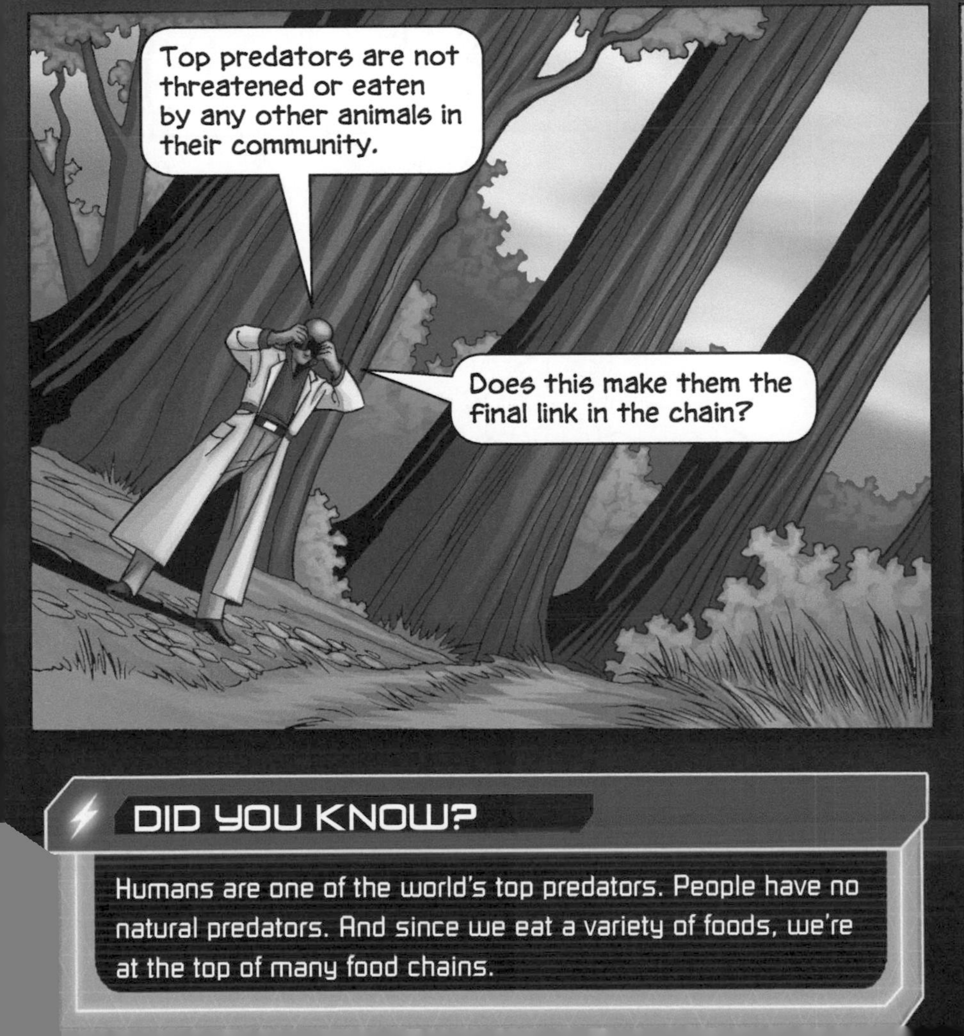
Top predators are not threatened or eaten by any other animals in their community.
Does this make them the final link in the chain?

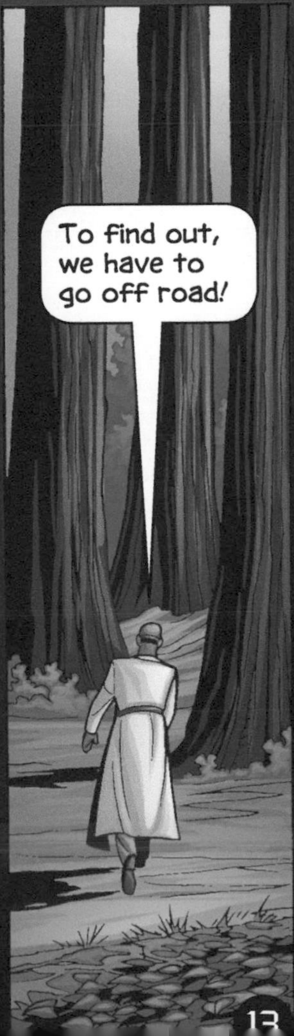
To find out, we have to go off road!

DID YOU KNOW?

Humans are one of the world's top predators. People have no natural predators. And since we eat a variety of foods, we're at the top of many food chains.

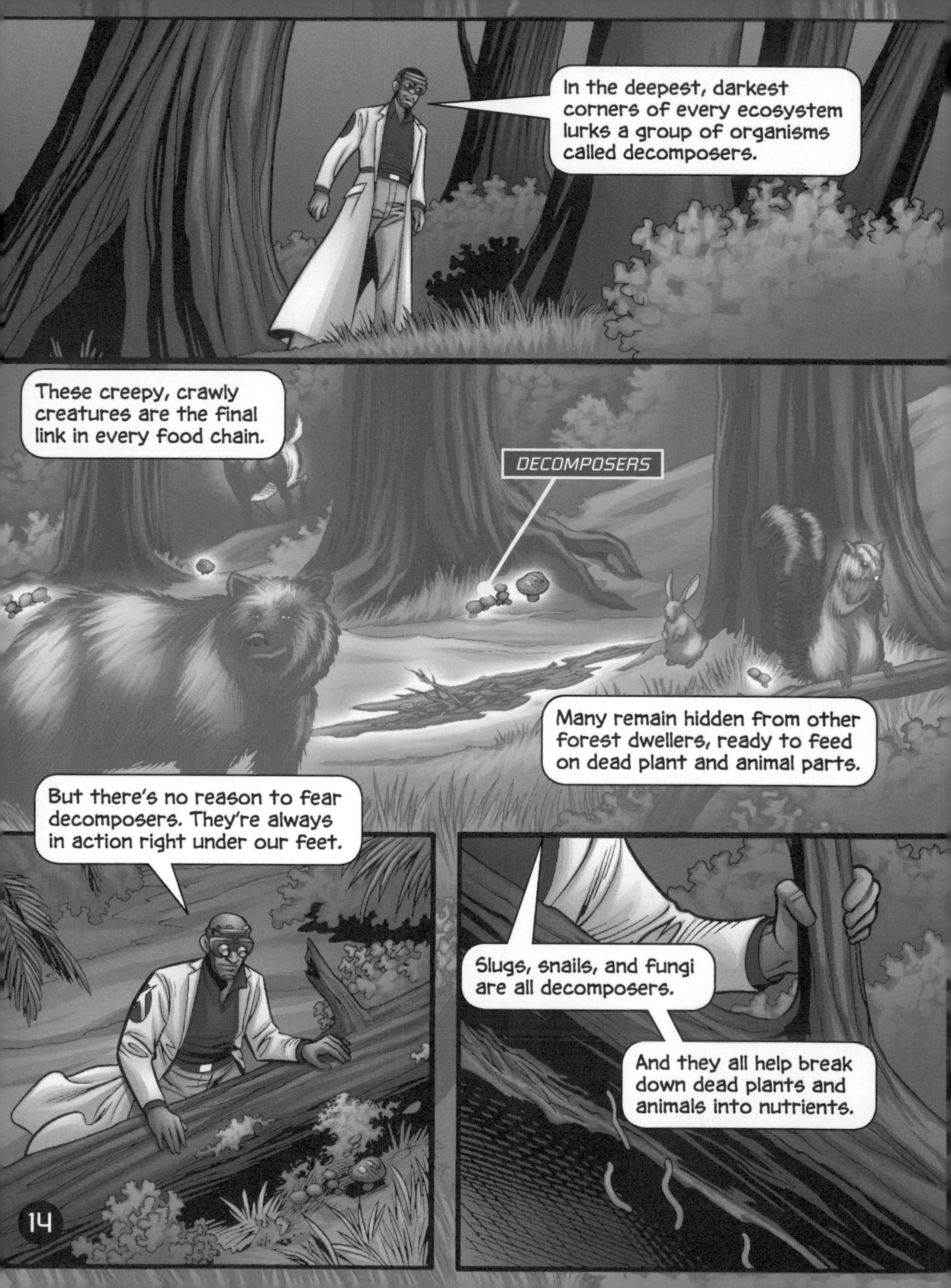
In the deepest, darkest corners of every ecosystem lurks a group of organisms called decomposers.
These creepy, crawly creatures are the final link in every food chain.
DECOMPOSERS
Many remain hidden from other forest dwellers, ready to feed on dead plant and animal parts.
But there's no reason to fear decomposers. They're always in action right under our feet.
Slugs, snails, and fungi are all decomposers.
And they all help break down dead plants and animals into nutrients.

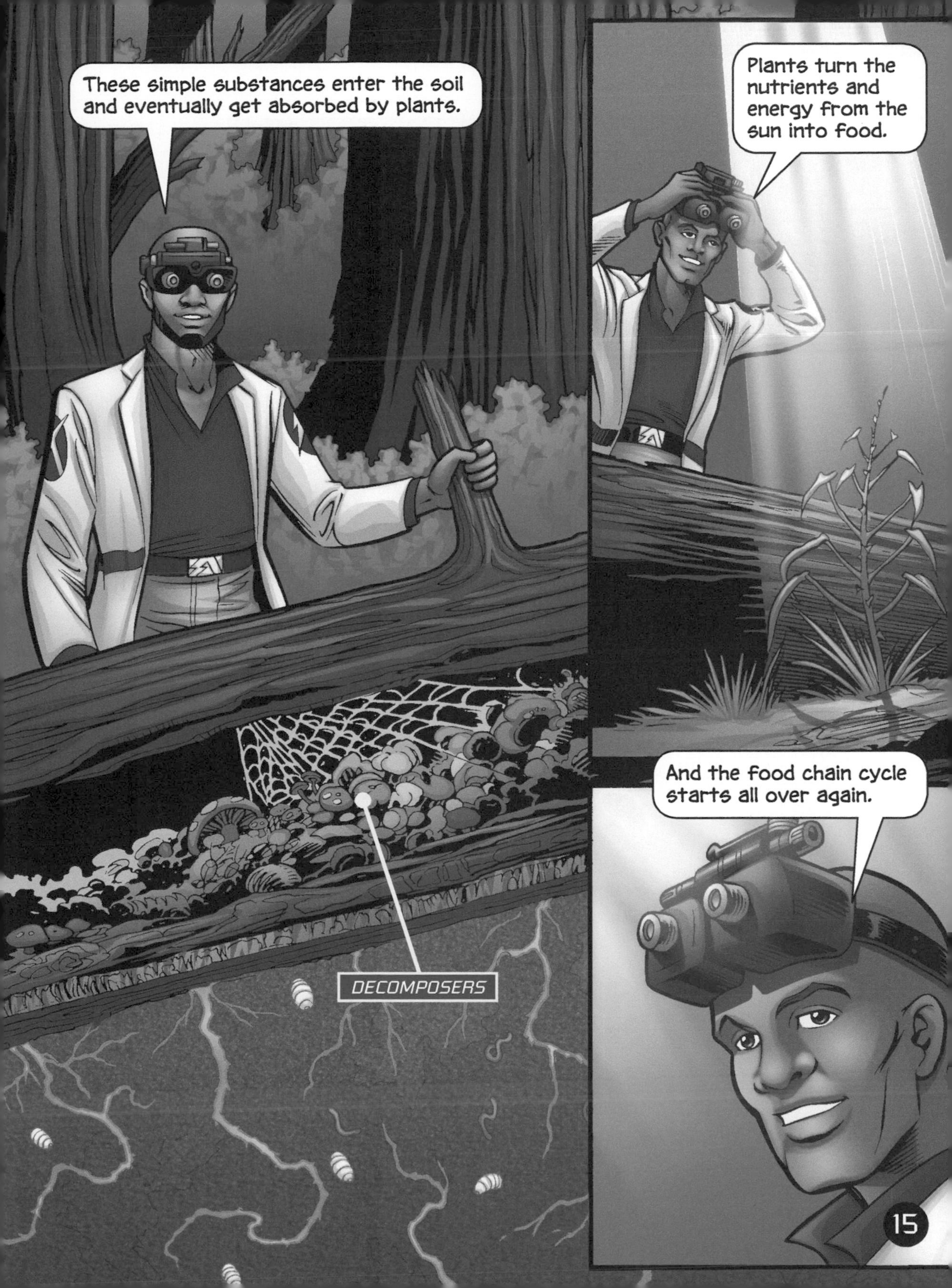

These simple substances enter the soil and eventually get absorbed by plants.
DECOMPOSERS
Plants turn the nutrients and energy from the sun into food.
And the food chain cycle starts all over again.

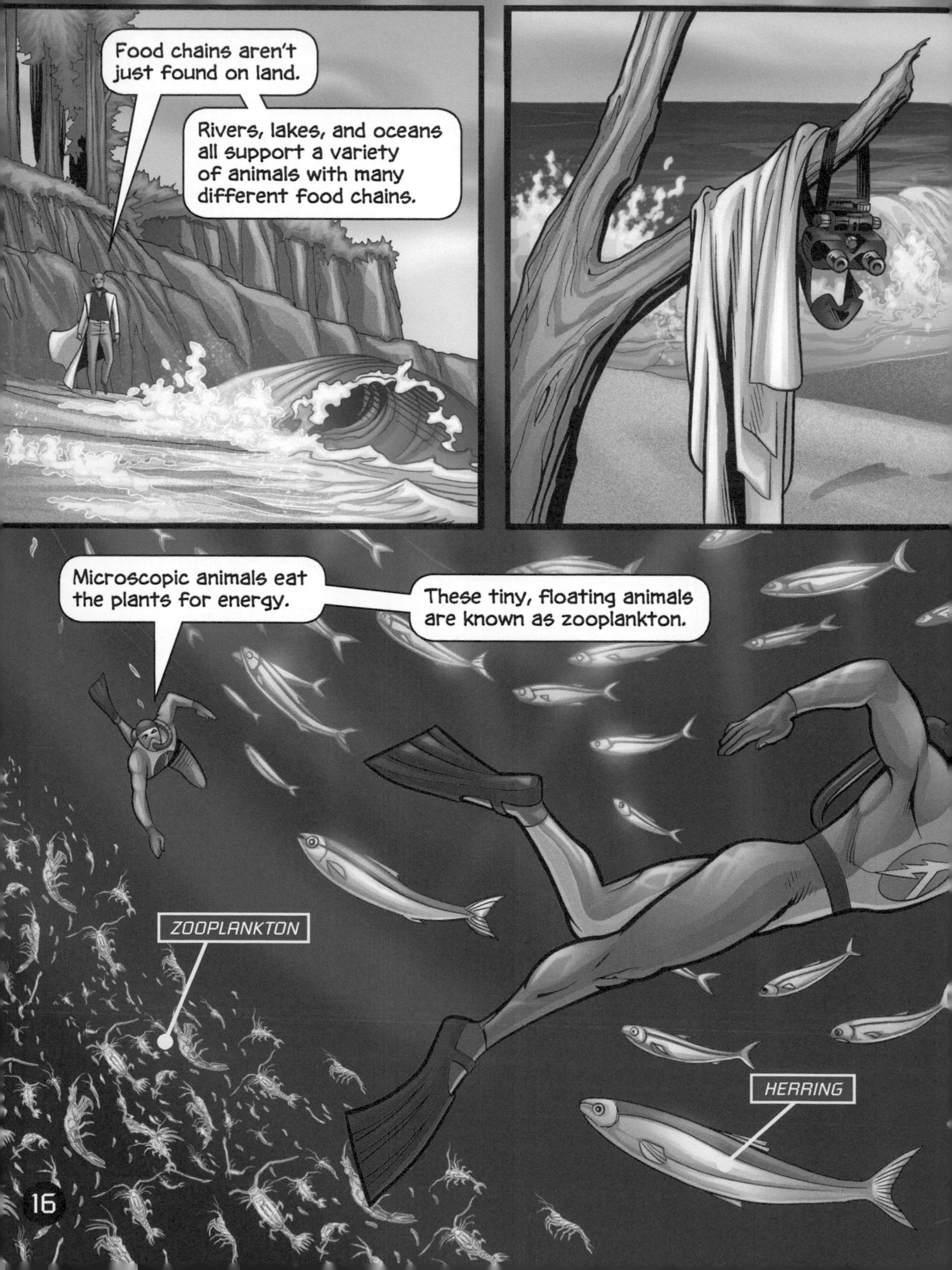
Food chains aren't just found on land.
Rivers, lakes, and oceans all support a variety of animals with many different food chains.
Microscopic animals eat the plants for energy.
These tiny, floating animals are known as zooplankton.
ZOOPLANKTON
HERRING

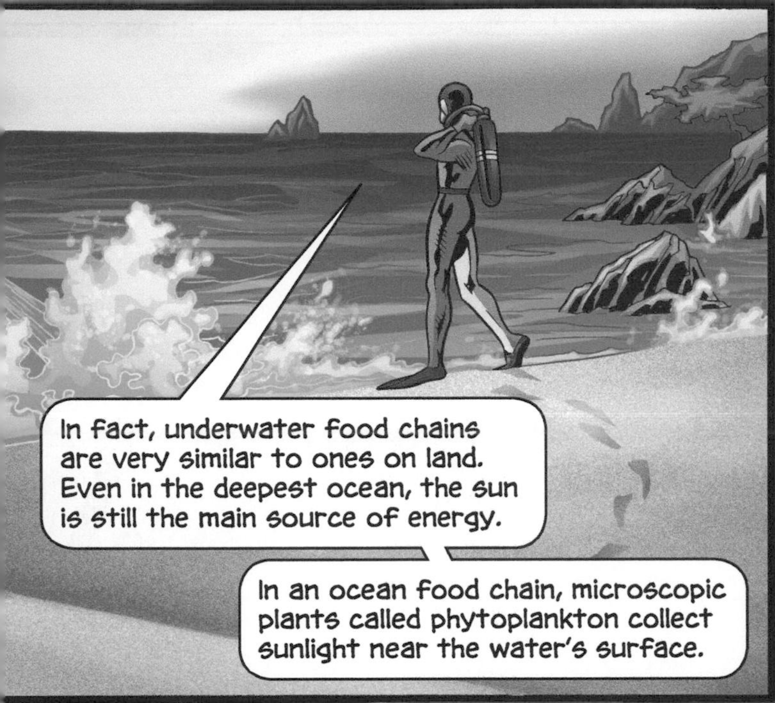
In fact, underwater food chains are very similar to ones on land. Even in the deepest ocean, the sun is still the main source of energy.
In an ocean food chain, microscopic plants called phytoplankton collect sunlight near the water's surface.

DEFINITION

Phytoplankton (fie-toh-PLANGK-tuhn) tiny plants that drift around and float in ocean waters

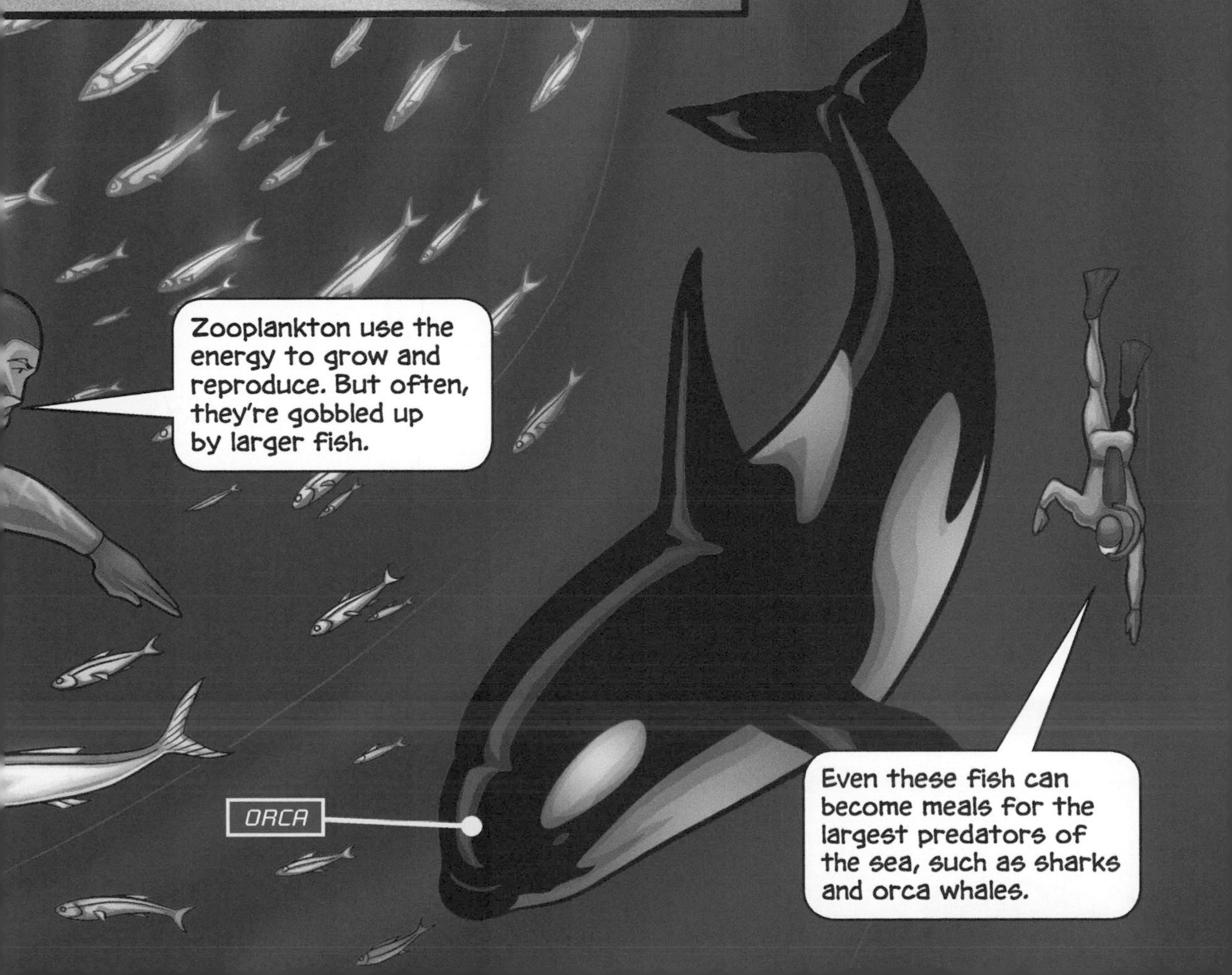
Zooplankton use the energy to grow and reproduce. But often, they're gobbled up by larger fish.
ORCA
Even these fish can become meals for the largest predators of the sea, such as sharks and orca whales.

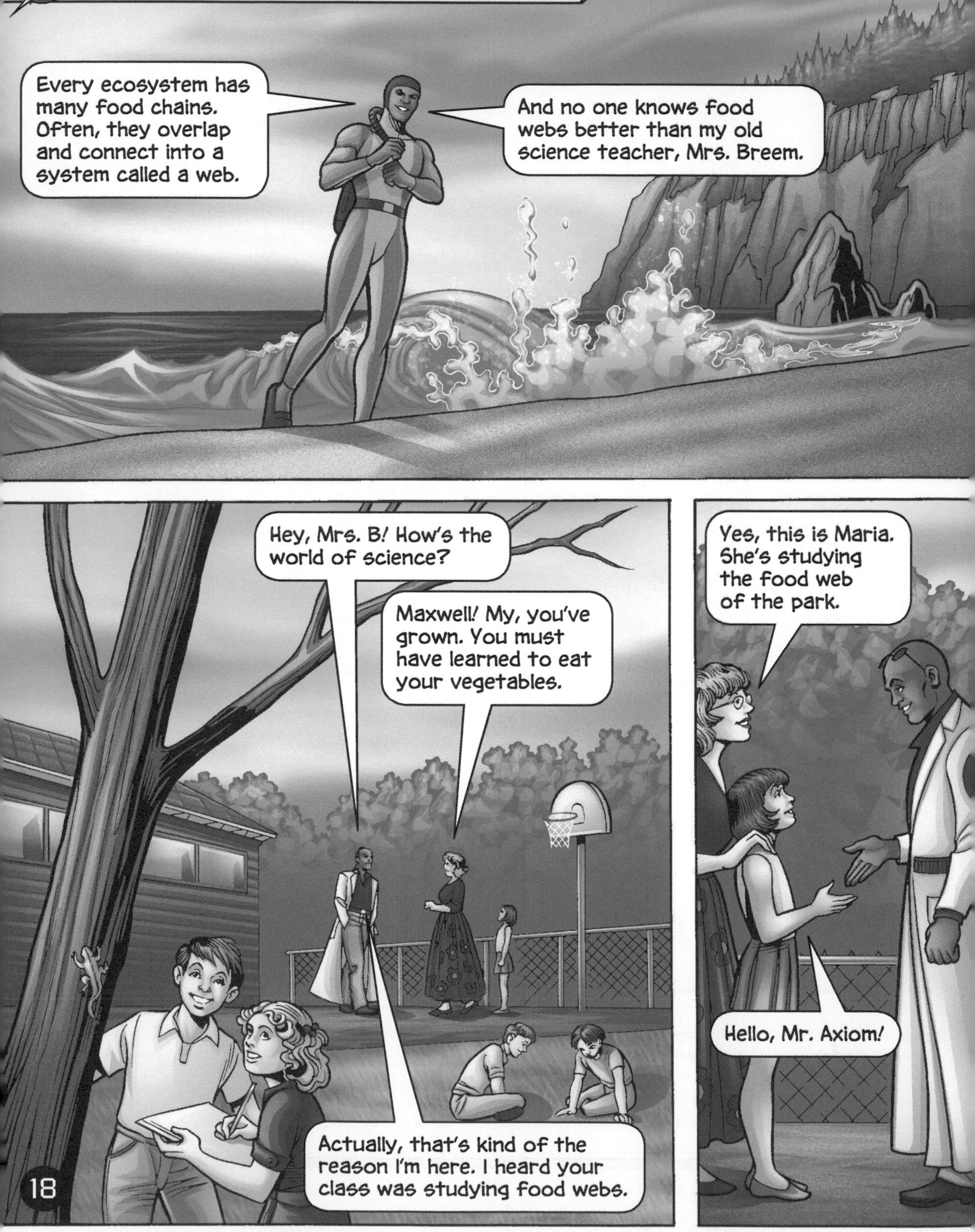
Every ecosystem has many food chains. Often, they overlap and connect into a system called a web.
And no one knows food webs better than my old science teacher, Mrs. Breem.
Hey, Mrs. B! How's the world of science?
Maxwell! My, you've grown. You must have learned to eat your vegetables.
Actually, that's kind of the reason I'm here. I heard your class was studying food webs.
Yes, this is Maria. She's studying the food web of the park.
Hello, Mr. Axiom!

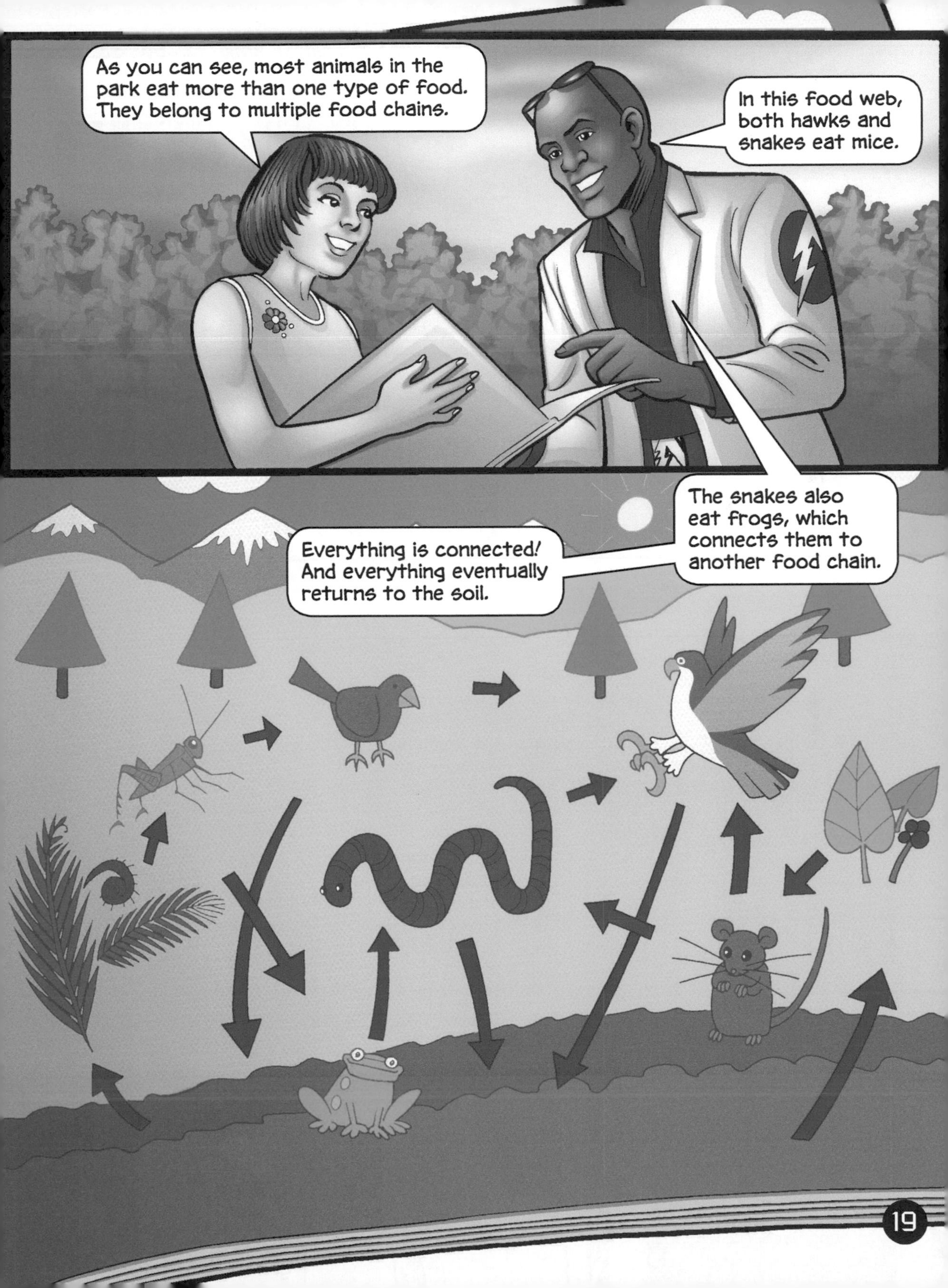
As you can see, most animals in the park eat more than one type of food. They belong to multiple food chains.
In this food web, both hawks and snakes eat mice.
Everything is connected! And everything eventually returns to the soil.
The snakes also eat frogs, which connects them to another food chain.

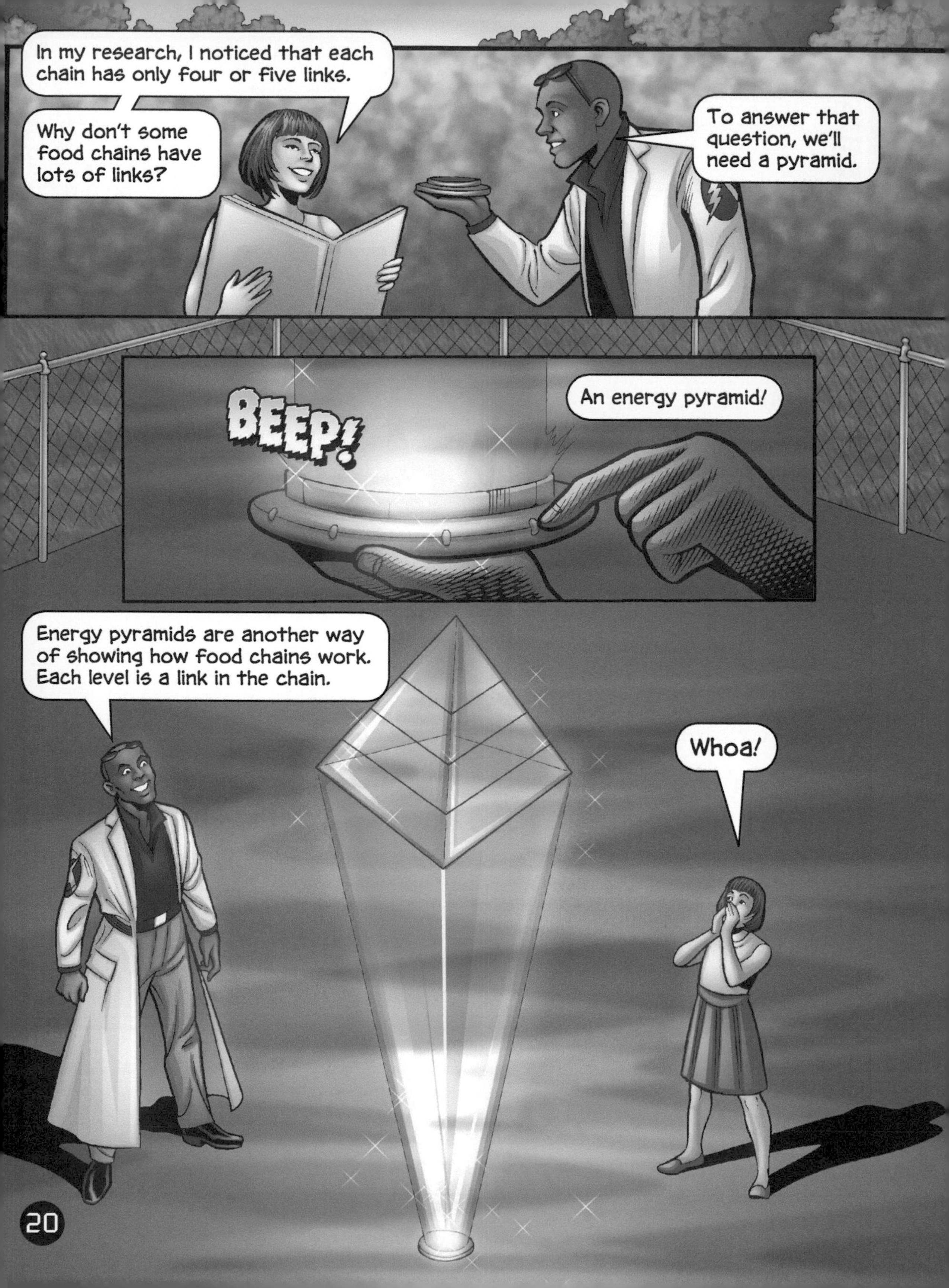
In my research, I noticed that each chain has only four or five links.
Why don't some food chains have lots of links?
To answer that question, we'll need a pyramid.
BEEP!
An energy pyramid!
Energy pyramids are another way of showing how food chains work. Each level is a link in the chain.
Whoa!

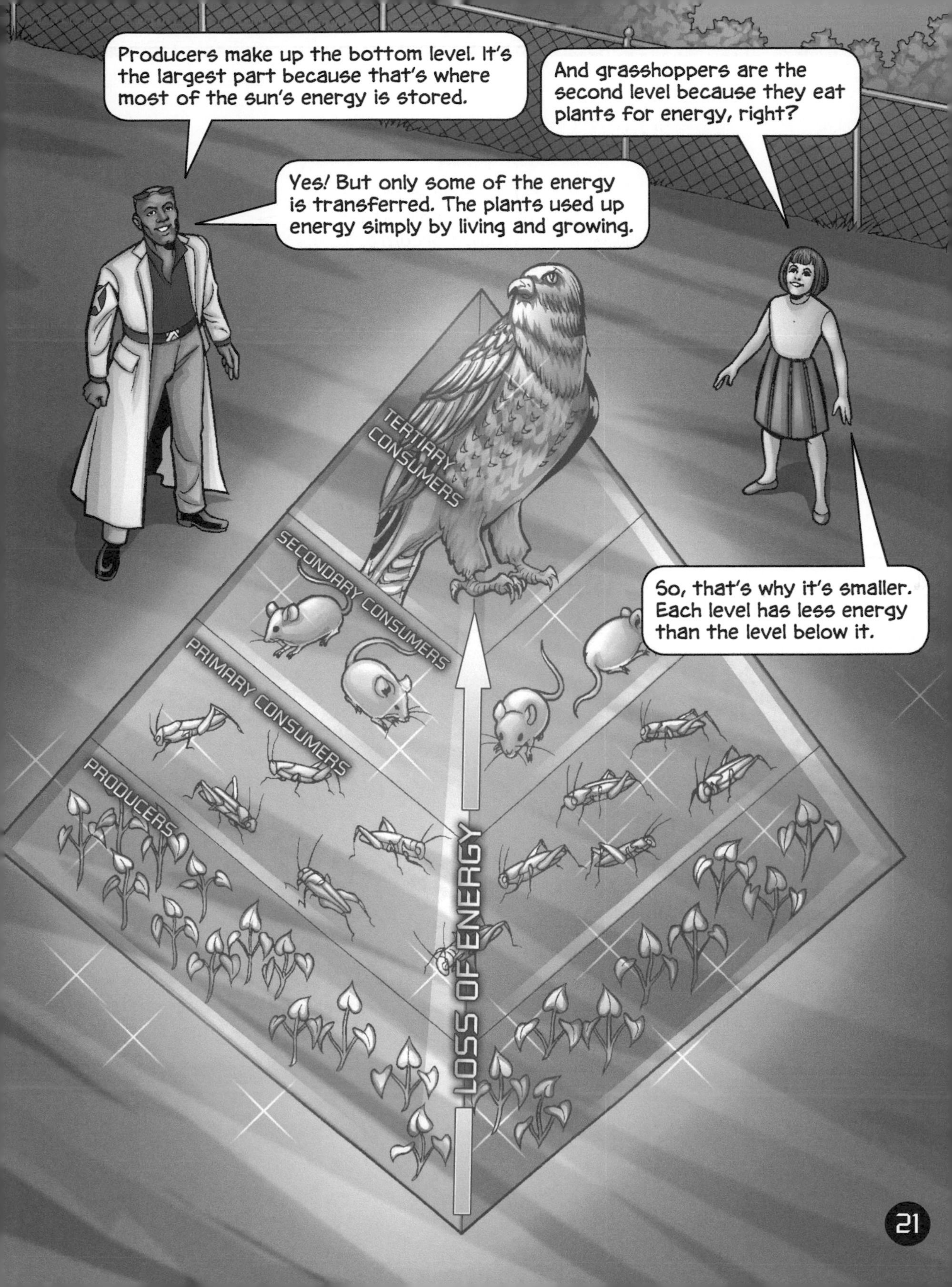

Producers make up the bottom level. It's the largest part because that's where most of the sun's energy is stored.
And grasshoppers are the second level because they eat plants for energy, right?
Yes! But only some of the energy is transferred. The plants used up energy simply by living and growing.
So, that's why it's smaller. Each level has less energy than the level below it.
TERTIARY CONSUMERS
SECONDARY CONSUMERS
PRIMARY CONSUMERS
PRODUCERS
LOSS OF ENERGY

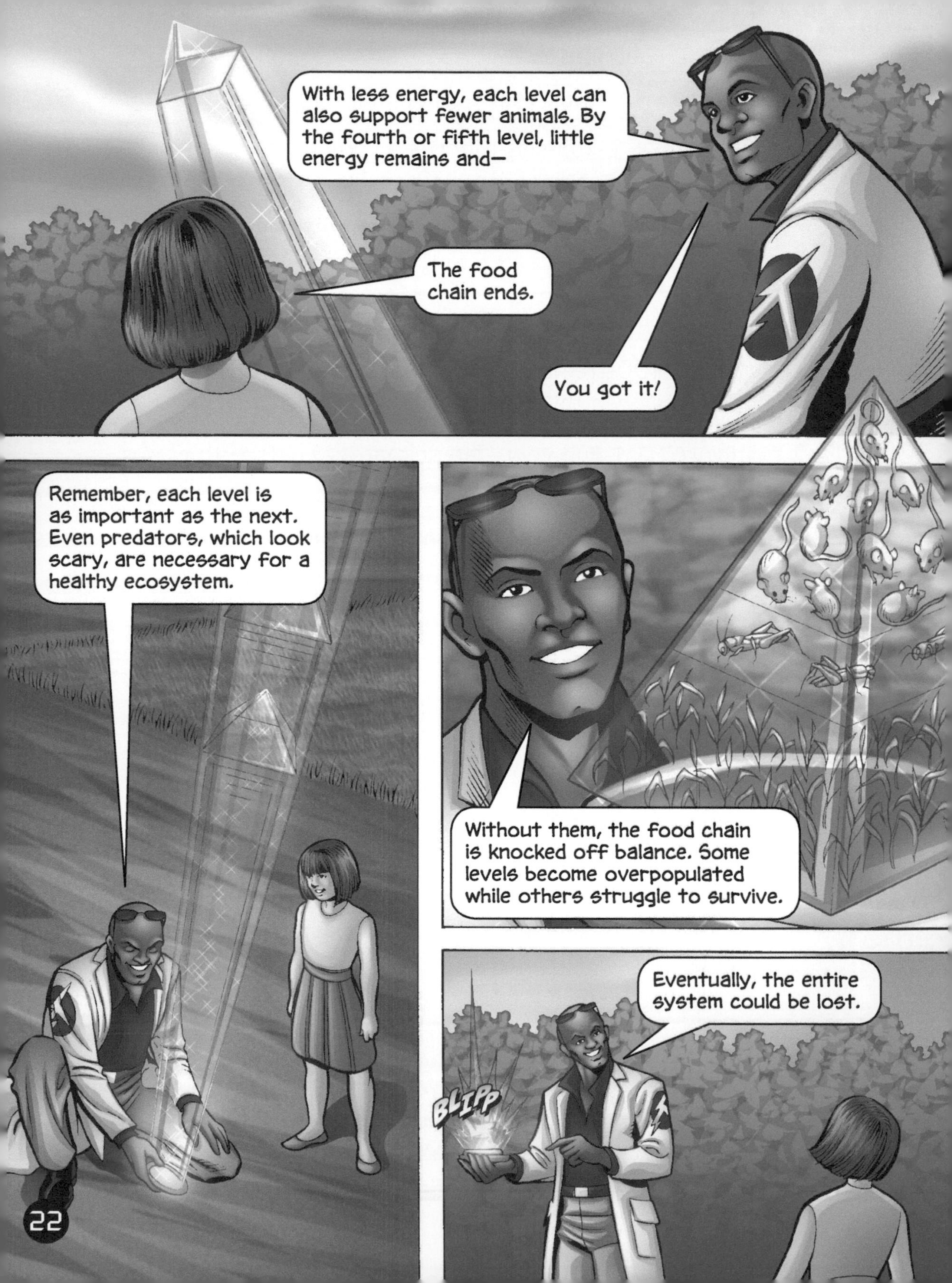
With less energy, each level can also support fewer animals. By the fourth or fifth level, little energy remains and—
The food chain ends.
You got it!
Remember, each level is as important as the next. Even predators, which look scary, are necessary for a healthy ecosystem.
Without them, the food chain is knocked off balance. Some levels become overpopulated while others struggle to survive.
Eventually, the entire system could be lost.
BLIPP

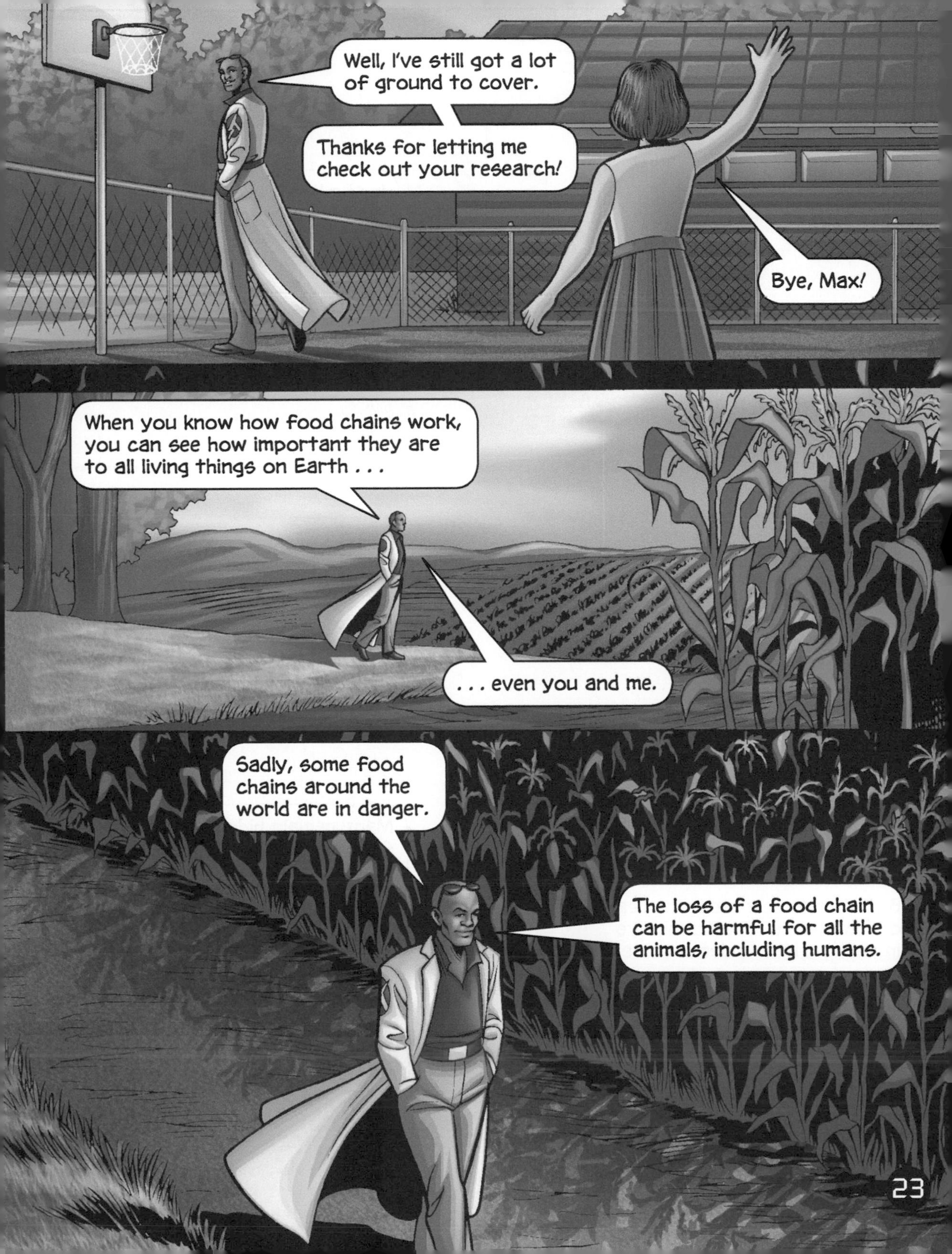
Well, I've still got a lot of ground to cover.
Thanks for letting me check out your research!
Bye, Max!
When you know how food chains work, you can see how important they are to all living things on Earth . . .
. . . even you and me.
Sadly, some food chains around the world are in danger.
The loss of a food chain can be harmful for all the animals, including humans.

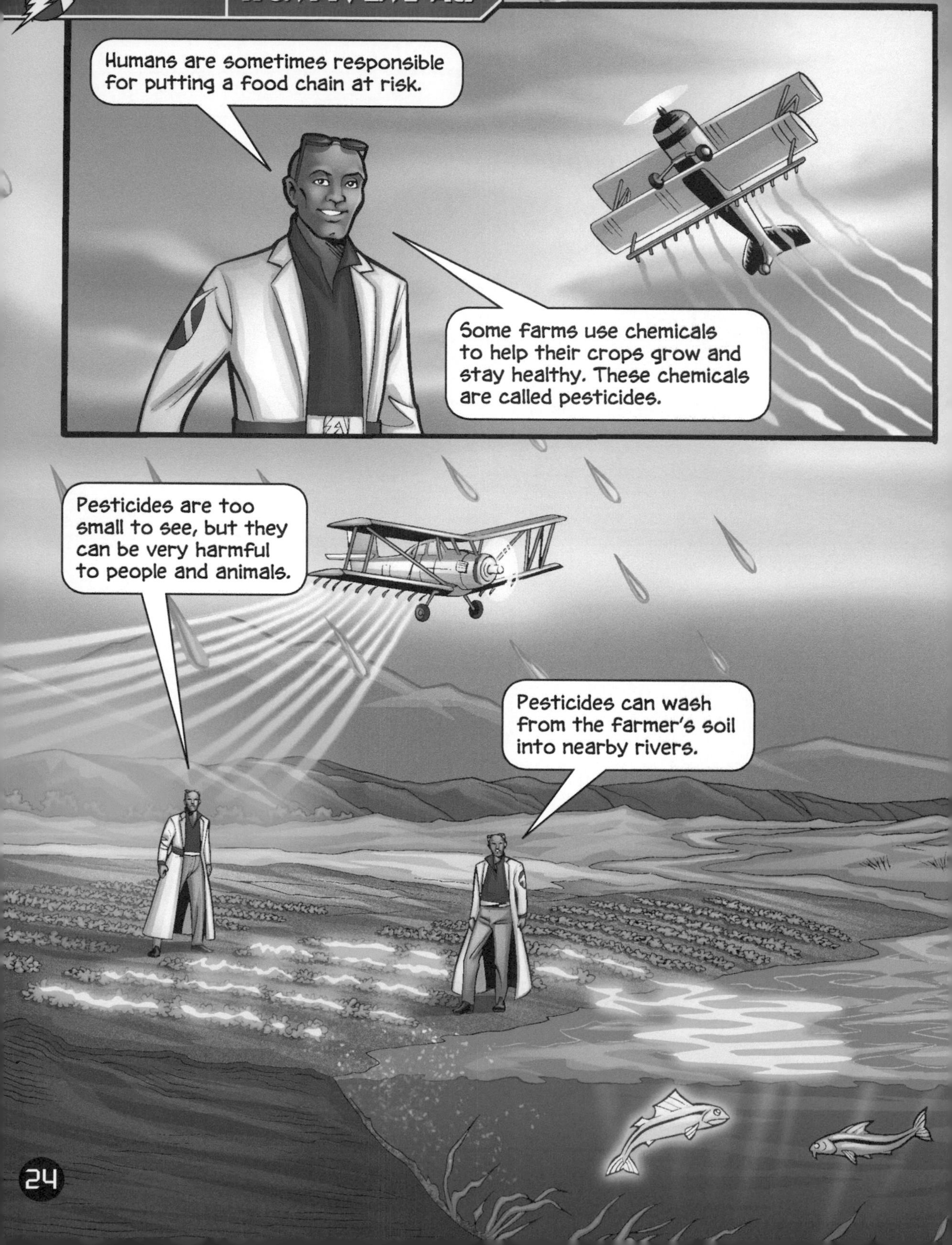
Humans are sometimes responsible for putting a food chain at risk.
Some farms use chemicals to help their crops grow and stay healthy. These chemicals are called pesticides.
Pesticides are too small to see, but they can be very harmful to people and animals.
Pesticides can wash from the farmer's soil into nearby rivers.

PEREGRINE FALCON

ACCESS GRANTED: MAX AXIOM

Even the fastest birds on Earth couldn't escape the impact of pesticides. In the 1940s, the number of peregrine falcons in the United States dropped dramatically. Scientists discovered that peregrines were consuming birds that had eaten insects contaminated with DDT. This pesticide had traveled up the food chain to the top predator. The DDT caused peregrine falcon eggs to thin and break before young could develop. Soon, the falcons were an endangered species. Thankfully, restrictions on DDT have helped the birds make a comeback. Today, they are no longer on the endangered list.

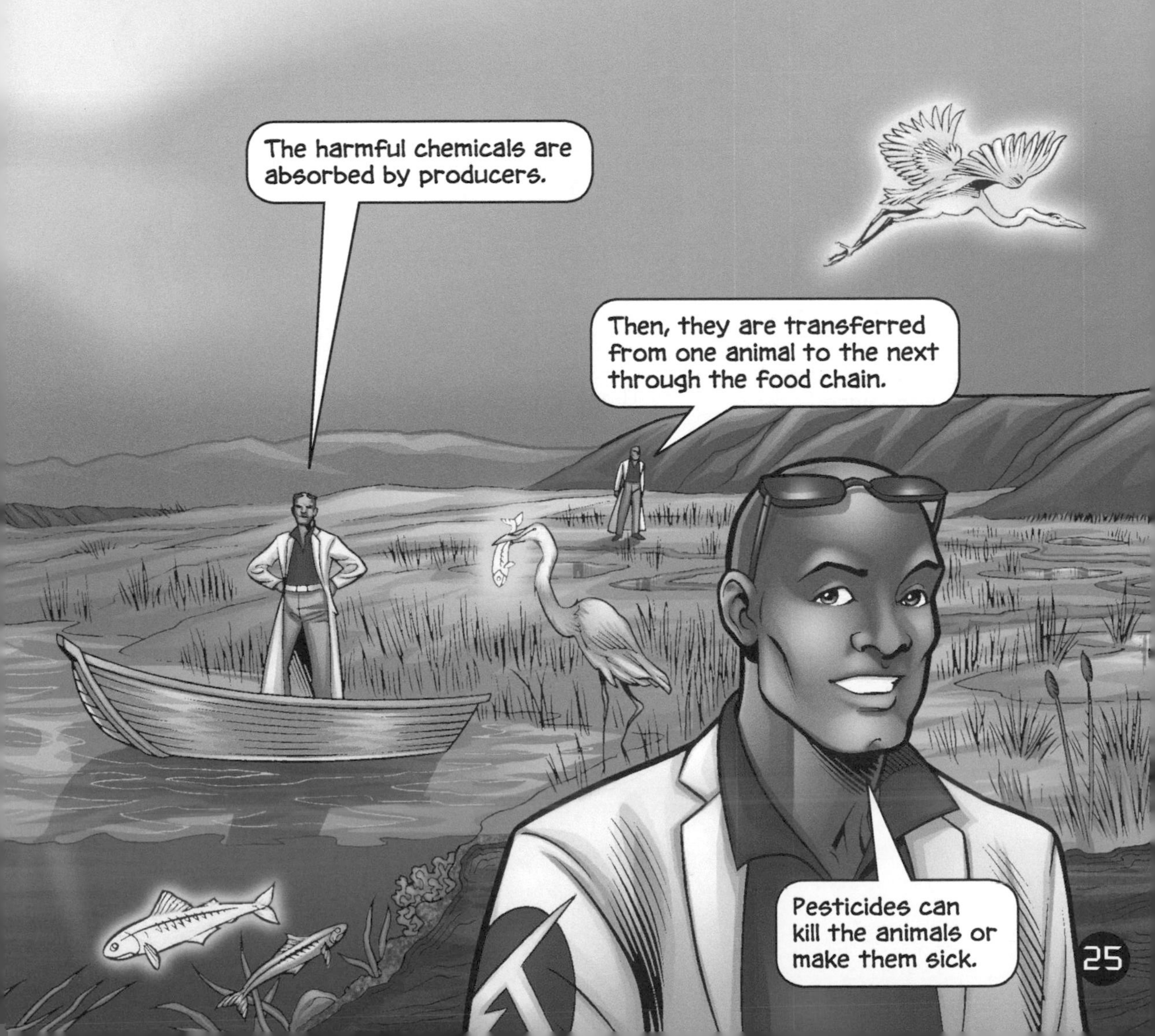

The harmful chemicals are absorbed by producers.
Then, they are transferred from one animal to the next through the food chain.
Pesticides can kill the animals or make them sick.

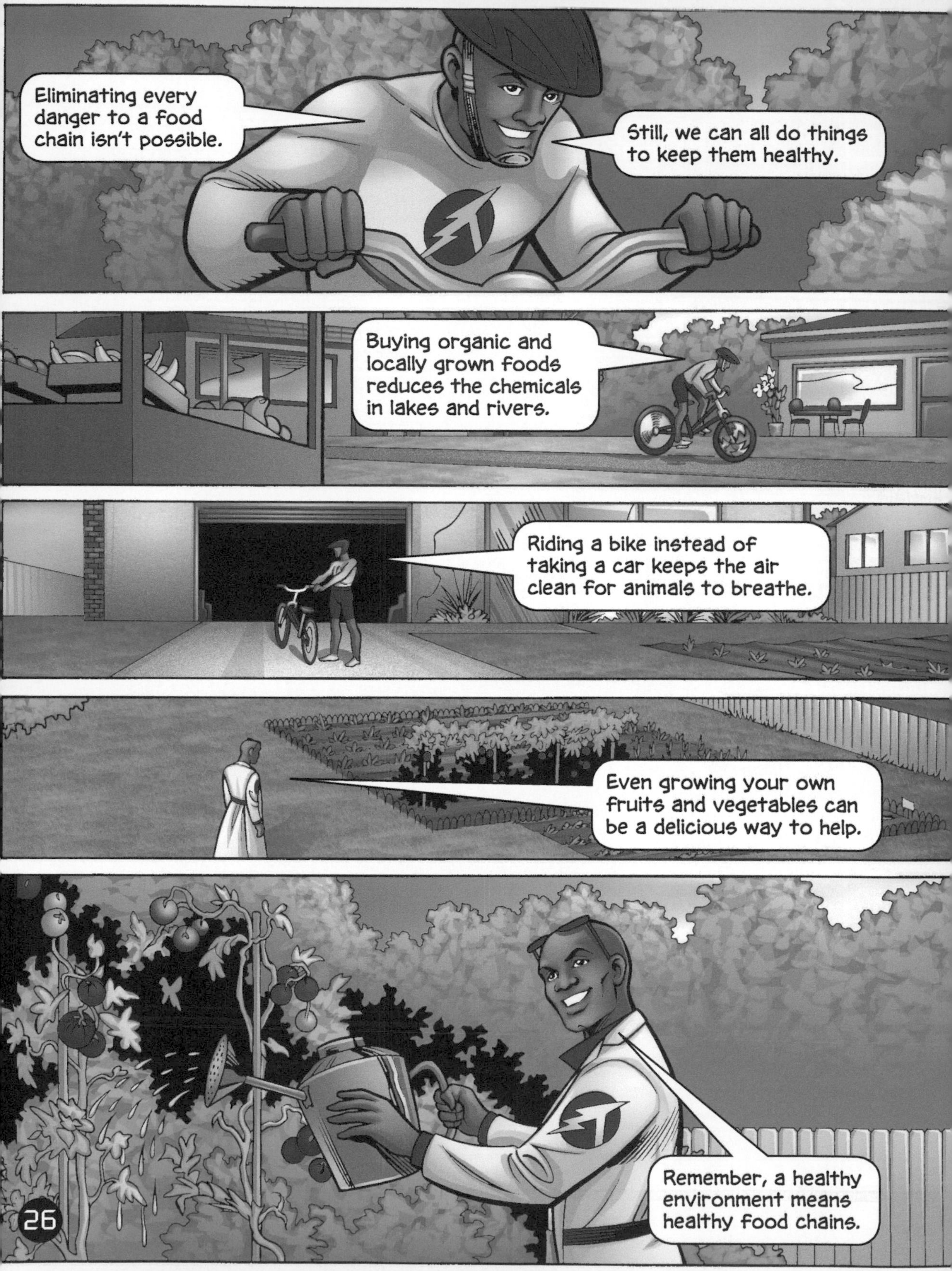
Eliminating every danger to a food chain isn't possible.
Still, we can all do things to keep them healthy.
Buying organic and locally grown foods reduces the chemicals in lakes and rivers.
Riding a bike instead of taking a car keeps the air clean for animals to breathe.
Even growing your own fruits and vegetables can be a delicious way to help.
Remember, a healthy environment means healthy food chains.

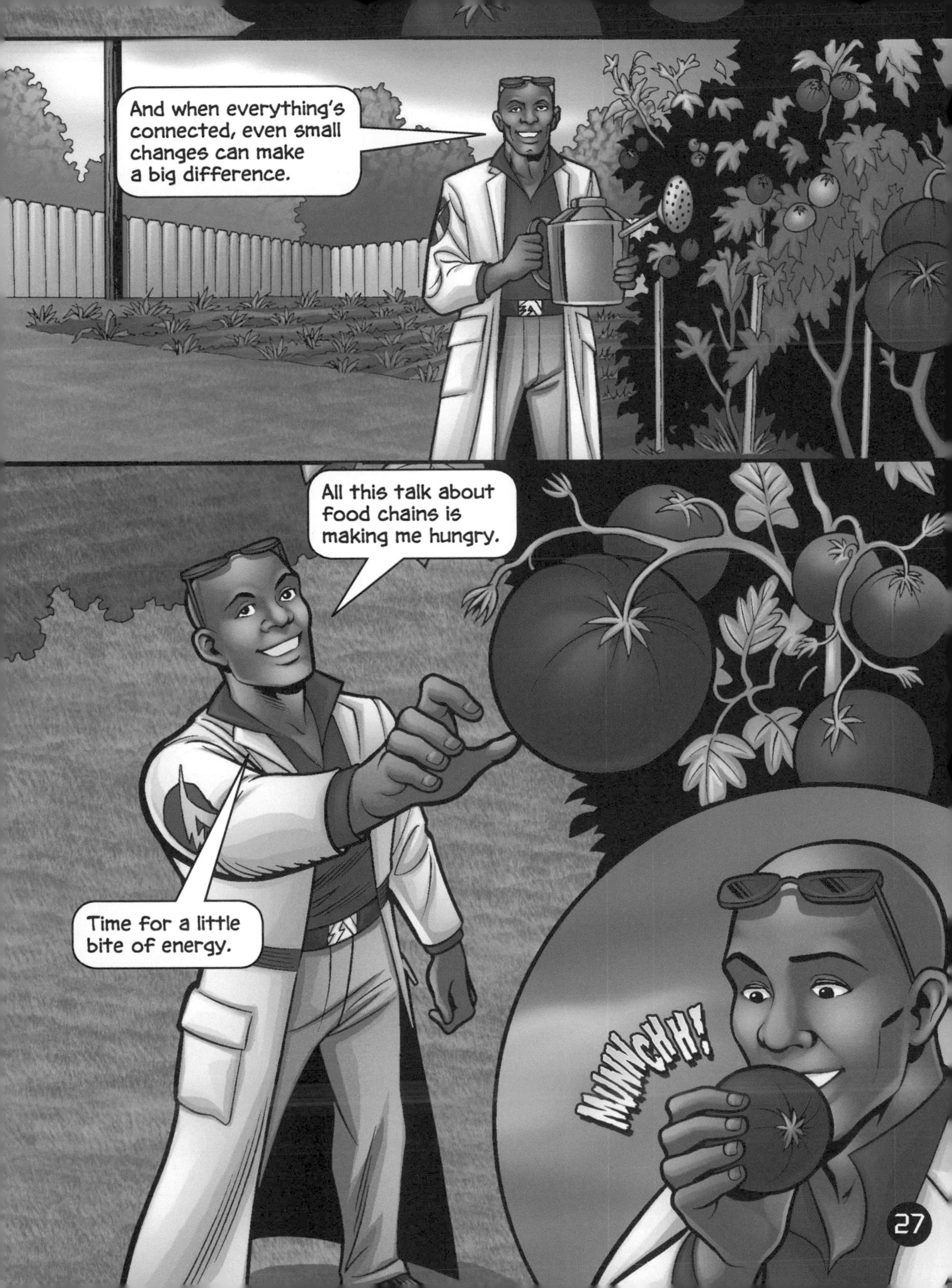
And when everything's connected, even small changes can make a big difference.
All this talk about food chains is making me hungry.
Time for a little bite of energy.
MUNNCHH!

FOOD CHAINS

An animal's mouth often determines its choice of foods. For example, some whales have strong teeth for eating large fish and seals. Other whales, such as the blue whale, have no teeth at all. Instead these gigantic mammals strain tiny organisms through a comblike series of plates, which hang from their upper jaw.

Some animals eat only one type of food every day! Koalas in Australia eat nothing but eucalyptus leaves. The koala's picky diet makes their habitat extremely fragile. If eucalyptus trees suddenly disappeared, koalas would have no other food to eat.

Many consumers have amazing abilities and features for capturing their prey. Cheetahs sprint 70 miles (113 kilometers) per hour to snag a rabbit or an antelope. Common loons dive more than 250 feet (76 meters) underwater in search of small fish or leeches. Spiders, such as the garden orb weaver, build strong webs to capture flying insects and even birds.

A parasite is an animal or plant that needs to live on or inside another animal or plant to survive. Parasites aren't usually listed on food chains or food webs. But even top predators can't escape these greedy creatures. Leeches are a parasite that will latch onto animals or humans for a tasty meal of blood.

Carnivores don't have to be large meat-eaters like lions or sharks. Plants can be carnivores as well. Venus flytraps, monkey cups, and other carnivorous plants live where nutrients in the soil are minimal. Instead, these types of plants get food by capturing small prey in their traps.

Wash what you eat! Farmers often spray vegetables and fruits with pesticides. These chemicals keep pests away in the field but can be harmful to people and animals. Rinsing produce before eating helps eliminate any remaining pesticides and reduces the chance of getting sick.

FOOD CHAIN GAME

Turn food chains into a game. Then test your knowledge or help a friend learn more about food chains!

WHAT YOU NEED:

paper and pencil
5 foam cups
colored permanent markers
15 small candies

grass   cricket   frog   snake   hawk

WHAT YOU DO:

1. Think about the wildlife in your neighborhood or nearby park. Write down a list of producers and consumers that live near you.

2. On your paper, draw a specific food chain that has 4-5 links. These will be the basis for your game.

3. Turn the foam cups upside down. Write the name of the lowest organism in your food chain along the rim of the first cup. Then decorate your cup from the rim up to reflect that organism.

4. Repeat step 3 with the other cups for the rest of your food chain. As you work, think about which cup represents the top predator and which ones are omnivores or carnivores.

5. Now stack your cups in order with your top predator at the top of the stack. Look at your food pyramid!

6. Unstack the cups and lay them out in a row in random order. Place 5 candies under the cup representing the lowest animal in your food chain. Place one less candy under each cup thereafter, leaving your top predator just one candy. The candies represent the transfer of energy in the food chain.

7. Find a friend who wants to play your game and have them guess how much "energy" belongs to each organism. Ask them to place the cups in the order of energy from smallest to largest. Don't give any hints!

8. Turn over the cups to reveal the energy for each animal. Then see if your friend can play at stacking the cups in their proper food chain order. Share the "energy" candies with your friend at the end.

DISCUSSION QUESTIONS

1. What is an energy pyramid? What does each level of an energy pyramid represent?

2. Can an organism belong to more than one food chain? Discuss why or why not.

3. How do the roles of plants and animals in a food chain differ? Discuss at least three differences.

4. What is the source of energy for producers? Discuss how their source is different from consumers in a food chain.

WRITING PROMPTS

1. What are food chains? Based on what you've read in the book, write a definition in your own words.

2. Draw a diagram showing the path energy takes from a plant to an animal and then to another animal. Label your diagram with what this path is called.

3. Pesticides affect some organisms in a food chain. Make a list of these organisms and briefly describe how they are affected.

4. Make a chart showing the different roles in a food chain. Write a short description of what each role does.

TAKE A QUIZ!

GLOSSARY

carnivore (KAR-nuh-vor)—an animal that eats only meat

ecosystem (EE-koh-siss-tuhm)—a community of animals and plants interacting with their environment

fungi (FUHN-jye)—organisms that have no leaves, flowers, or roots; mushrooms and molds are fungi.

herbivore (HUR-buh-vor)—an animal that eats only plants

nutrient (NOO-tree-uhnt)—a substance needed by a living thing to stay healthy

omnivore (OM-nuh-vor)—an animal that eats both plants and other animals

organic (or-GAN-ik)—using only natural products and no chemicals or pesticides

organism (OR-guh-niz-uhm)—a living plant or animal

pesticide (PESS-tuh-side)—a chemical used to kill insects and other pests that eat crops

predator (PRED-uh-tur)—an animal that hunts other animals for food

prey (PRAY)—an animal hunted by another animal for food

tertiary (TUHR-shee-air-ee)—of third rank, importance, or value

READ MORE

Hardyman, Robyn. *Exploring Food Chains with Math*. Math Attack: Exploring Life Science With Math. New York: Rosen Publishing, 2017.

O'Donnell, Liam. *Understanding Photosynthesis with Max Axiom, Super Scientist: An Augmented Reading Science Experience*. Graphic Science 4D. Mankato, Minn.: Capstone Press, 2018.

Pettiford, Rebecca. *Coral Reef Food Chains*. Who Eats What? Minneapolis, Minn.: Jump!, Inc., 2017.

Tarbox, A.D. *A Rainforest Food Chain*. Odysseys in Nature. Mankato, Minn., 2016.

INTERNET SITES

Use Facthound to find Internet sites related to this book.

Visit *www.facthound.com*

Just type in 9781543529517 and go!

INDEX